The Joy of Good News

The Joy *of* Good News

Mort Crim

Servant Publications
Ann Arbor, Michigan

Vine Books is an imprint of Servant Publications especially designed to serve evangelical Christians.

Published by Servant Publications
P.O. Box 8617
Ann Arbor, Michigan 48107

Cover design by Eric Walljasper
Author photograph: Bob Foran, Ann Arbor, Michigan

01 02 03 04 10 9 8 7 6 5 4 3 2 1

Printed in the United States of America
ISBN 1-56955-245-2

Library of Congress Cataloging-in-Publication Data

Crim, Mort.
    The joy of good news / Mort Crim.
        p. cm.
    ISBN 1-56955-245-2 (alk. paper)
    1. Christian life. I. Title.

BV4510.3 C75 2001
248.4—dc21

                                        2001016236

*Dedicated with love and admiration
to the memory of*

Alvah Crim
Vera Martin
Floyd Bowman

Three champions of the faith whose ministries
brought joy to many and who now know
the *ultimate joy*.

Abbreviations

GNMM	Good News for Modern Man
NAB	New American Bible
NIV	New International Version
NJB	New Jerusalem Bible
NRSV	New Revised Standard Version
RSV	Revised Standard Version
NLT	New Living Translation

Preface

Comedian George Carlin said he would start jogging just as soon as he saw a runner who was smiling. Some people feel that way about Christianity. They might consider becoming a Christian if they could ever see one smiling. Strange, isn't it, that a faith that begins with a proclamation of joy to the world seems to produce so *many* long faces! If the average nonbeliever were given a word association test, the word "Christian" might trigger such terms as "rules," "creeds," "self-denial," "pious," or "stodgy." Rarely would it evoke the word "joy." Why? Are real Christians truly the hapless, brooding victims of a burdensome set of regulations? Or are we simply the misunderstood victims of bad PR?

It's impossible, of course, to generalize about Christians any more than to generalize about Republicans, Democrats, African Americans, journalists, teachers, scientists, or any other group. Unfortunately, some Christians do fit the cheerless stereotype. But to live without joy is to miss the main point of Jesus' life and message. He understood that rules are necessary if life is to be lived well. However, he made it clear that strict observance of good rules *alone* would never produce joy.

To live life *abundantly*, he said, it's necessary to know God. And the Good News is that through Jesus it's possible to see this mysterious, invisible person we call God. But more than merely see—it's possible to relate to God. To experience God. To know God in a very personal way.

The Good News should produce the most incredible joy imaginable. The problem is that this basic, simple truth sometimes becomes lost in a haze of ecclesiastical mumbo jumbo. We can become so preoccupied with the rules, regulations, and technical interpretations of our faith that its essence is obscured. And when we lose the essence, we lose the joy.

In sports, a good coach is constantly reminding the team, "Don't forget the basics." In football the most sophisticated plays ever devised won't win a game if the players forget how to run, block, and tackle. Similarly, a life of faith only produces joy if we "don't forget the basics." And joy is not to be confused with fun, pleasure, or even happiness.

For example, I recall going to dinner with friends a few weeks after my father died. They thought, and rightly so, that I needed some diversion. I needed to get my mind off the persistent sadness of that loss. I remember having fun that night. But I certainly didn't feel joy. Look around you. Lots of people are having fun whose lives are anything but joyous. We can engage in activities that are fun—and we should. Many healthy, wholesome activities in life will bring us pleasure. That's great.

But joy is unique. It isn't the same kind of momentary feeling we get from having fun or engaging in some pleasurable activity. It's deeper, more profound than that. Joy is produced by relationships. It's what we feel when that tiny baby son or daughter grasps our finger for the first time. It's what we feel when we reminisce about the parents we've loved or about that *special friend*. It's what we feel when we're madly in love and she says, "Yes, I'll marry you." Whatever else joy is, it's inevitably tied to relationships.

That's why Christians should be the most joyous people on earth. Because our faith is based not upon doing everything right, but upon a right relationship. Our joy springs from the sure knowledge that Jesus was God's special representative to humans. That his life mirrored what the mysterious and invisible Creator is really like. That his teachings and his example provide us with a better guide for living than a whole library full of rules and regulations.

As Christians, our joy doesn't come from our relationship to a particular church, doctrine, or religious point of view. It comes, as joy always does, from a personal relationship. A relationship to the One who said, "If anyone loves me, he will obey my teaching. My Father will love him, and we will come to him and make our home with him" (Jn 14:23 NIV).

Acknowledgments

Thousands of people have touched my life over the years and in so doing have influenced my thoughts, my philosophy, and this book. They include members of my family, teachers, ministers, missionaries, colleagues, and even strangers. It is, of course, not possible to thank them individually.

However, a few people have made specific and significant contributions to *The Joy of Good News* and I want to publicly thank them:

My wife, Renee, who pledged when we married that she would "simplify" my life and who continues to nobly pursue that elusive objective. I am more grateful than she can know for her patience, her support, her editorial critiques—and most of all, her willingness to endure the stress my heavy writing, broadcasting, and speaking schedule places upon both of us.

My most able and congenial assistant, Cindy Carney, who's given up on ever simplifying my life but who does a magnificent job of making the crazy pieces fit. She manages on a daily basis to make some sense out of the chaos which seems endemic to my chosen profession.

Terry Oprea, president of *Mort Crim Communications, Inc.*, who has been with me—spiritually and professionally—from the beginning and, I suspect, will be there 'til the end.

Jeff Tottis, executive vice president and chief financial officer of our company. A good guy who's raised "bean counting" to an art form.

My children, Al and Carey, who think for themselves, who frequently disagree with me on matters of faith and "meaning," but whose intellectual challenges I welcome because they serve to sharpen my own thinking and, from time to time, have even forced me to reevaluate my own conclusions. I also thank Al for his dedicated research and superb writing skills that make my *impossible* workload possible.

A special thanks to those loyal and hard-working members of our radio syndication team, Suzanne Gougherty and Lisa Hubbs. And, to other members of the greatest communications organization ever assembled:

Chris Heaton, Tim Hinkle, Daphne Hughes, Kim Kasinec, Paul Manzella, Geri Neal, John Owens, Bob Rossbach, Cassandra Smith, and Greg Zonca.

It was a distinct honor to have portions of this manuscript read by a former publisher of the Detroit Free Press who is also one of the nation's most compelling storytellers. Neal Shine's suggestions were constructive and helpful and I valued them just as I value his friendship.

Finally, a super thank-you to my good friend and editor, Bert Ghezzi, who conceived the idea of this series of *Good News* books. Bert's expertise as both editor and accomplished author in his own right has contributed immeasurably to this work. Bert, you know how much I appreciate you.

And to everybody at Servant Publications—Thanks and keep up the *good works!*

A Good Motto

*I*t was the post-Depression years. Money was still tight. Mother was determined that my father would complete his college studies, but paying tuition, buying food, and raising a child—me—was an incredible challenge. At that time grandparents also took care of grandchildren voluntarily and not just because of a marriage break-up. The nuclear family was still a reality, especially in the small, southern Illinois town where I was born. So, while Mother and Dad set off for Indiana to pursue his studies for the ministry, I remained at the family home with my father's parents.

My grandfather was a judge and my grandmother, a former English teacher. Everybody in the family called them "Mom and Dad Crim," so I did, too. I never called them grandma or grandpa. Since both of my mother's parents were dead, I never knew a "grandma" or a "grandpa."

Mom Crim was a devout Christian with a great sense of humor. Her three passions in life were her church, her family, and the English language. In her later years, she loved to recall how her "little Mort" used to preach when he was about four or five years old. There was no television in the early 1940s, but everybody had a radio in the living room. Most radios came with a bench so one could sit in front of it and listen to Jack Benny, Bob Hope, *Fibber McGee and Molly,* or the *Lone Ranger.* According to Mom Crim, she once saw me standing behind the radio bench as though it were a pulpit, preaching to one of my neighborhood friends. Mom said she almost lost it when I pounded my small fist on the bench and proclaimed, "And if you say 'ain't' and other bad words, you'll go to hell." Apparently, I gave Mom's admonitions about grammar the same standing as her theology.

Mom and Dad Crim's house was comfortable but modest. It wouldn't have qualified for a pictorial spread in *Architectural Digest,* but it was a warm, inviting place that reflected my grandparents' love of God and family. Photographs on table-tops and dressers gave strong testimony to the pride and devotion they felt for their children and grandchildren.

And Mom's mottoes told anyone who entered the house how she felt about God. I'm not sure where she bought them—probably some catalogue—but they weren't very attractive. Cheap looking, actually. Cardboard signs with a blue background and silver-colored letters stamped in, a single hole punched in the top where the mottoes could be hung on a nail. No frames. Just cheesy-looking cards strategically placed on living room walls where no visitor could miss them.

Despite their aesthetic deficiencies, those mottoes were very important to Mom Crim because they expressed her most fundamental beliefs about life. Each motto contained a portion of Scripture. And one of them had a profound influence upon my young life.

A few years ago, a newspaper columnist was interviewing me about my career in television. We were having lunch. He put his fork down, paused for a long time, looked me in the eye, and said, "Mort, help me understand something. As a journalist, you've seen the worst that life can dish out, yet you remain the eternal optimist. It doesn't fit. What am I missing? Journalists are supposed to be cynics."

For some reason the question stirred memories of my early childhood. And suddenly I remembered one of Mom's mottoes. When I was too young to read, I had asked her one day what it said. She not only read it to me, but helped me to memorize it. It said: "All things work together for good to those who love God."

That, I told my columnist friend, was the source of my optimism. The belief instilled in me so early in life, that our existence is not an accident. That life didn't happen by random chance. That there is a Creator. And that if we do our part, ultimately everything will come out all right.

Mom Crim believed—and I believe—that in the end it does all work out in the way it's supposed to when we put our trust in God.

Mom's motto is my earliest recollection of the Good News. The memory still fills me with joy.

> *The Lord will keep you from all harm—he will watch over your life.*
> *The Lord will watch over your coming and going both now and forevermore.*
> PSALM 121:7-8 NIV

Mysteries of Faith

> *The joy of all mysteries is the certainty that comes from their contemplation, that there are many doors yet for the soul to open on her upward and inward way.*
>
> —ARTHUR CHRISTOPHER BENSON

What causes the light to come on when you flip the switch? How does a gasoline combustion engine work? How does a television set or a FAX machine convert pictures into electronic impulses, then back into pictures again? How do airplanes fly? How do microchips work?

Some of us may be able to answer some of these questions. Some of the questions may leave us completely clueless. What's interesting is that we can make use of all these devices even if we're totally ignorant of how they work. You don't have to be an electrician to turn on a light. You don't have to be a mechanic to drive a car. You don't have to be an electronics expert to watch TV or send a fax. People who don't know the first thing about aeronautical science fly in airplanes all the time. And computer illiterates such as I routinely use computers and often use them with great skill.

What's the lesson in all this? The lesson is that we don't have to understand the "mystery" of how something works in order to benefit from it.

It's the same with our Christian faith. It's practical. It works. Life functions better when we follow Jesus. When we follow his example, act on his principles, we're more effective at the business of living. We're happier. More optimistic. Our relationships are healthier. When we pray, we discover that things happen. Sometimes circumstances seem to change. Sometimes we change. Whichever occurs, it's clear that when we pray, something happens.

How does all this work? Don't ask me. I'm no theologian. I'm a *user,* not an *expert.* All I know is that my own life and other lives that I observe are infinitely better because of faith.

As a journalist, I've been trained to observe, analyze, and report. For several years, I covered the manned space program at Cape Canaveral. It wasn't necessary for me to understand fully the science of rocketry in order to observe, analyze, and report on what was happening. Similarly, I don't have to possess any deep, profound knowledge about the *hows and whys* of faith to recognize that wherever it's present, life is demonstrably and unarguably improved.

In what way? Two words come immediately to mind: Peace and joy. These are two qualities that seem sadly missing from a majority of lives today, but strangely present in the lives of believers. Why is this so? Again, I have no adequate, technical explanation. Nor is one necessary. It's simply demonstrable. Observable. Provable.

If you want academic answers, consult a theologian. If you want to know how a computer works, talk to my stepson, Jeff. He's an expert programmer. But if you simply want to know whether faith or computers work, talk to me. I can't explain either, but I've experienced both and can confirm that they do work!

If you thought those questions about electricity, cars, airplanes, and computers were tough, try these:

Why do innocent children die of horrible diseases? Why are they slaughtered in wars? Shot to death in random acts of violence? Why are some babies born deformed? Why is there so much cruelty and suffering in the world? How can a God who is both all-powerful and all-loving permit senseless tragedies? Now these are mind-numbing questions. We'll all be experts in computers before we have any adequate answers to them. After all, they've challenged and troubled the minds of the best theologians and philosophers for thousands of years.

Truthfully, there is no rational answer to such questions. But we humans, with our logical minds and our pragmatic temperaments, continue struggling with them as though somehow, we'll finally solve the riddles. This intellectual dilemma must have been what Jesus had in mind when he promised to provide a "peace that passes understanding." It is a peace that comes with a profound faith—a faith that doesn't defy reason, but also doesn't depend upon reason for all the answers. A faith that acknowledges mystery. A faith that concedes not everything can be figured out.

When we finally and fully accept faith with all its mystery, we discover the peace beyond human understanding. Perhaps that is why people of faith so often seem to overflow with that other rare quality, *joy*. It is only when we are able to trust the contradictions of life to the Creator of life that we can experience true and sustained joy. As long as we're butting our heads against the wall of logic, trying to penetrate life's mysteries with our own brains, we'll be continually frustrated. But when we accept, by faith, the One who is *the answer* we no longer have to have all the answers.

That acceptance brings us a peace beyond understanding. And a joy, unspeakable.

How does it work? Beats me.

> *For now we see in a mirror dimly, but then face to face. Now I know in part; then I shall understand fully, even as I have been fully understood.*
>
> 1 CORINTHIANS 13:12 RSV

The Joy of a Second Chance

Love is an endless act of forgiveness, a tender look which becomes a habit.

—PETER USTINOV

*I*s there anyone who hasn't messed up somewhere, sometime?

Sometimes we are the hardest on ourselves. It may be easier for us to forgive or overlook the mistakes of others than our own.

Ed McManus publishes a periodical called *The Jokesmith,* and he can tell some wonderfully funny anecdotes. But once in awhile Ed comes across a touching or poignant story. This is such an account.

It's a story he heard a priest tell in Puerto Rico about a woman dying from AIDS. The priest was called in to comfort her, but nothing he could say seemed to help.

"I'm lost," she kept repeating. "I've ruined my life and every life around me. Now I'm going painfully to hell and there's no hope for me."

The priest noticed a framed picture of a pretty girl on the dresser. "Who's this?" he asked.

The woman immediately brightened. "She's my daughter, the one beautiful thing in my life."

"And would you help her if she was in trouble, or made a mistake? Would you forgive her? Would you still love her?"

"Of course I would!" the woman replied. "I would do anything for her. Why do you ask such a question?"

"Because I want you to know," the priest said, "that God has a picture of *you* on *His* dresser."

Is it unreasonable to extend to ourselves the same understanding, forgiveness, and acceptance that we so easily and naturally offer our children?

> As far as the east is from the west,
>   so far he removes our transgressions from us.
> As a father has compassion on his children,
>   so the Lord has compassion for those who
>   fear him.
>
> PSALM 103:12-13 NRSV

Techie Kindness

> *Three things in life are important: The first is to be kind. The second is to be kind. And the third is to be kind.*
>
> —HENRY JAMES
>
> *A man wrapped up inside himself makes a very small bundle.*
>
> —BENJAMIN FRANKLIN

*A*re computers stripping us of our humanity? Are we becoming simply numbers assigned by corporations? Not if David McC. can help it. He runs a computer for a major health care system. These are his words:

"Walter died last Tuesday. And Mary had a baby. I didn't know Walter or Mary, but I thought of them. Walter reminded me of my own grandfather whom I still love and miss after thirty-two years. Mary reminded me of my wife. And the sweet look on her face when our children were born. I wondered if Mary's husband was there. I wondered if Walter died alone.

"It's my job to make sure the computer processes and pays hospital claims correctly. Sometimes, late at night, when I am alone with the computer, I stop a claim. I just look at it. It helps me remember why I am here. And what is important.

"Walter: If you are in heaven, say hello to Grandpa.

"Mary, I hope your little girl brings you joy.

"Someday, when she is older, tell her that someone she doesn't even know thought of her the day she was born. And cried."

Technology is only a tool. If we lose the human touch, it won't be the computer's fault. It will be ours.

> *Love one another deeply from the heart.*
>
> 1 PETER 1:22 NRSV

Essential Joy

> *Simplicity, clarity, singleness: these are the attributes that give our lives power and vividness and joy.*
>
> —RICHARD HALLOWAY

I'm something of a gadget nut and I almost never visit a hardware store without buying something. Just this week I discovered one of these purchases near my workbench and, so help me, I can't remember what it's for, what it's supposed to do, or why I bought it. Must have seemed like a good idea at the time.

How many things do we accumulate in our lives that we don't really need? And how many necessities do we take for granted?

Recently, at a famous resort, I interviewed a member of the president's cabinet who had been invited there to make a speech. Would he spend the night, I wondered?

No, he said with a smile. "My thirteen-year-old daughter is in a program this evening back in Washington. I have to be there for that."

Relaxing, golfing, or politicking at that resort no doubt were attractive options, but for this man, they were the gadgets of life, not the essentials.

The TV in the den—that's a gadget. The warm touch at the door that says, without words, "It's nice to have you home"—that's a necessity.

Ultimately the quality of our lives isn't determined by how many things we've plugged into the wall, parked in the garage, hung in the closet, or tossed onto the workbench. Ultimately the quality of our lives is determined by how we define *necessities.*

> *The kingdom of heaven is like treasure hidden in a field. When a man found it, he hid it again, and then in his joy went and sold all that he had and bought that field.*
>
> MATTHEW 13:44 NIV

Mistaken Judgment

> *Forebear to judge, for we are sinners all.*
> —WILLIAM SHAKESPEARE

A small boy walked into the ice cream store and sat alone at a table. The waitress put a glass of water in front of him and asked rather sharply what he wanted.

"How much is a hot fudge sundae?" the boy asked.

"Three dollars," she said.

The boy pulled a couple of dollars out of his pocket along with some change, counting it all. Then he asked, "Well, how much is plain ice cream?"

By now other customers were waiting and the waitress was growing impatient. "Two fifty" she said, clearly irritated.

Again the child counted his money and then said, "Okay, I'll just have the dish of chocolate ice cream." She brought it, literally slamming it down in front of the boy, then walked off without a word. The boy finished the ice cream, paid his check at the counter, and left.

It was only when she went back to clear the child's table that the waitress understood why he couldn't buy the hot fudge sundae. There, neatly counted out on his table were a quarter, two dimes, and a nickel. It was her tip.

Judging people is always risky. Prejudging them is downright foolhardy.

> *Judge not,... For with the judgment you pronounce you will be judged, and the measure you give will be the measure you get.*
>
> MATTHEW 7:1-2 RSV

The Joy of Home

A house is no home unless it contain food for the mind as well as for the body.

—MARGARET FULLER

*T*he traditional American home has been under siege for several years and yet it survives because no one has yet come up with a better, more effective replacement. Recently I came across a writing by Norman Corwin, who—perhaps better than anyone I've read—captures the unique qualities which make home such a special place.

With ten books, home becomes partly a library. Three pictures make it a little museum. Old forgotten letters, pictures, and souvenirs make the attic or basement a wing of archaeology. One big crowded closet, a warehouse.

A piano or violin may make the home a part-time conservatory. Grace at mealtime, or answering a child's questions about God, can turn home into a church, a synagogue, or a mosque.

In the throes of argument, home is a court. In sickness, a field hospital. A TV screen makes home a theater. When kids climb trees, fences, or forbidden high furniture, home becomes a commando camp.

One child makes it a course in liberal education. Three children may turn it into a campus.

Home? There's never been anything created that's quite like it.

So long as the home remains a strong repository of all that's good and valuable in the world, just so long will there be reason to hope for our future.

> *Kindness and faithful love pursue me*
> *every day of my life.*
> *I make my home in the house of Yahweh*
> *for all time to come.*
>
> PSALM 23:6 NJB

From the Mouths of Babes

If you can't be a good example, then you'll just have to be a horrible warning.

—CATHERINE AIRD

I hope that over the years I've taught my children a few things. Sharing wisdom gained from life's experiences certainly is a parent's responsibility. But the teaching isn't one-way. I know I've learned more than a few lessons from my children.

Eastman Chemical's CEO, Earnie Deavenport, tells about a Little League coach who called one of his young players aside and said, "Son, do you understand what cooperation is? What a team is?" The little boy nodded.

"Do you understand that what matters is whether we win together as a team?" The child nodded that he did.

"So," the coach continued, "when a strike is called, or you're out at first, you don't argue with the umpire or curse him or attack him. Do you understand all that?" The little boy indicated that he did.

"Good," the coach said. "Now go over there and explain it to your mother."

Wisdom isn't always a matter of age. Sometimes our children are the students, sometimes, the teacher.

Those who are peacemakers will plant seeds of peace and reap a harvest of goodness.

JAMES 3:18 NLT

The Joy of Forgiveness

> Hate is a prolonged form of suicide.
> —DOUGLAS V. STEERE
>
> There is no point in burying a hatchet if you're going to put up a marker on the site.
> —SYDNEY HARRIS

As the young woman stepped into the phone booth, she said to the man waiting to use it, "Don't worry. I'm only going to be in here long enough to hang up on him." Throughout our lives there will be people who make us want to hang up on them, or worse. People who hurt us. Insult us. Cheat us. Betray us.

Our first thought may be to get back at them. But grudges are among life's heaviest loads and usually it's the person who carries one who ultimately suffers the most. It was that great philosopher, Buddy Hackett, who said he'd learned how foolish it is to carry a grudge. *Because while you're hating your enemy, your enemy is out dancing.* Maybe instead of getting mad or getting even we simply get on with our lives.

To carry a resentment gives our enemies power over us they don't deserve. It allows our enemies to dictate how we feel. The feeling is never very good. To forgive is to set a prisoner free and then to discover that the prisoner is you.

To forgive doesn't mean to forget. What it does mean is to let go. A grudge will always bite the hand that feeds it.

> "Lord, how often shall my brother sin against me, and I forgive him? As many as seven times?" Jesus said to him, "I do not say to you seven times, but seventy times seven."
>
> MATTHEW 18:21-22 RSV

Choosing Happiness

> *Most folks are about as happy as they make up their minds to be.*
>
> —ABRAHAM LINCOLN

*T*hey say laughter is good medicine. They're right.

Dom DeLuise has spent much of his life making other people laugh. But for him, the laughter hasn't always been a two-way street. Often while he was joking on the outside, he was tormented on the inside by depression.

At one of his lowest points, Dom DeLuise felt hopeless—that life was useless. Then came Christmas. And when his little boy asked, "Dad, what do you want for Christmas?" DeLuise replied, "Happiness. I want happiness and you can't give it to me."

Well, on Christmas day, this little sixty-pound child handed his father a piece of cardboard with the word *happiness* scrawled on it.

He said, "You see, Dad, I can give you happiness."

It was like someone had turned on a light. The love and concern of an innocent child suddenly lifted the gloom. Dom DeLuise says he laughed. He cried. He was once again ready to live.

Perhaps that's why he spends so much time visiting sick children in hospitals. After all, it was the love of a child that brought joy back into his life. Now, his humor brings joy into the lives of other children. What goes around comes around.

"Being able to make people laugh who aren't feeling well—it's like a gift from God," Dom DeLuise says.

Love and laughter are potent medicine—better than two aspirin and a phone call in the morning. And they work a lot faster.

> *Happy are those whose greatest desire is to do what God requires:*
> *God will satisfy them fully!*
> *Happy are those who are merciful to others:*
> *God will be merciful to them.*
>
> MATTHEW 5:6-7 GNMM

The Joy of Change

*H*ow many reasons do you have for putting off what you want to do? Fear? Timing? Your age? The cost? We can find dozens of excuses and sometimes we just need a little incentive to push us over the edge of our own hesitation.

Abraham Lincoln had a favorite story about a frog, mired in a deep, muddy, wagon track. His frog friends tried and tried to coax him out, but he just couldn't do it. He was stuck. Finally they all gave up and left him there. To their great surprise, the next day they found the frog by the pond, chipper and alert and most pleased with himself.

One of his frog friends said, "How did you get here? We thought you couldn't get out of that rut."

And the frog said, "I couldn't. But a wagon was coming so I had to."

When our desire to do or be or accomplish something becomes so strong that we simply *have* to, then we'll do it. And not one of our excuses will be sufficient to keep us mired in the rut. Until then, all the urging in the world won't get us unstuck.

You've been telling your family and friends all the reasons why you can't make a change in your life. Maybe they believe you. The important question is: Do you really believe those reasons yourself?

> *Turn from your sins and turn to God, because the Kingdom of Heaven is near.... Prove by the way you live that you have really turned from your sins and turned to God.*
>
> MATTHEW 3:2, 8 NLT

The Joy of Keeping On

> *To me, old age is always fifteen years older than I am.*
>
> —BERNARD BARUCH

*O*peration Able is dedicated to the proposition that ability is ageless and that older people are among our most valuable—and most wasted—resources. They believe it's better to wear out than to rust out. So each year Operation Able honors seniors who keep on keeping on, like Ed C., special assistant to the president at Edward C. Levy Company. Ed's been with Levy since 1960, and according to his boss, Ed's only failure was trying to retire—three times. He's eighty-six now and still working hard every day.

Jim G. has worked since he learned to plow at age seven. Now, at eighty-five, he's accounts receivable courier for Sherwood Food Distributors, with a successful collection rate of 96 percent.

Rose M.? She's eighty-five, and shows up every day at the Botsford Continuing Care Corporation to work in therapy. Rose always brings with her a smile, a laugh, a hug, a hand to hold, and a shoulder to cry on.

So next time you're feeling a little on the ancient side, think again. For some folks, the real fun doesn't begin until they hit sixty-five. They're the ones who never seem to age. Maybe it's because they don't have time to grow old.

For those who maintain enthusiasm and purpose into their later years, being over the hill simply means having a better view.

> *Even when I am old and gray, do not forsake me, O God, till I declare your power to the next generation.*
>
> PSALM 71:18 NIV

Sound Judgment

The faults in others that irritate us the most may be the ones we recognize within ourselves. Of course, we don't always recognize them, as this story shows.

A husband was quite concerned about his wife's hearing. On his next visit to the doctor, he asked for suggestions. He explained that his wife never seemed to hear him the first time and he was always having to repeat things.

The doctor had an idea. When the man got home, he should stand about fifteen feet from his wife, say something, and if she didn't respond, move a few feet closer and say it again. He was to keep moving in until she heard him. That way he'd have a better idea about the severity of his wife's deafness.

Sounded like a plan. So that evening he did exactly as the doctor had suggested. Standing about fifteen feet behind his wife he said, "Honey, what's for dinner?" Hearing no response, he moved closer. Asked again, "What's for dinner?"

Still no answer. Finally he moved right up to her and, only

inches away, he asked again, "Honey, what's for dinner?"

And she said, "For the third time, I said vegetable stew."

There are times when what we think is somebody else's problem actually turns out to be our own. And there's no better way to forget the faults of others than to remember our own.

> But who can detect his own failings?
> Wash away my hidden faults.
> And from pride preserve your servant,
> never let it be my master.
>
> PSALM 19:12-13 NJB

A Healthy Perspective

> *Conquering any difficulty always gives one a secret joy, for it means pushing back a boundary-line and adding to one's liberty.*
> —Henri Frederic Amiel

Erik was barely fourteen when he joined his high school wrestling team in Phoenix. Soon, he was named cocaptain. And not long after that, he became state champion runner-up in his class. Erik was born to be competitive. Mostly he competed with himself, taking on personal challenges, such as rock climbing. In 1995, he scaled Mount McKinley—at twenty-thousand feet, the highest peak in North America. Then he took on the three thousand-foot granite monolith, El Capitan, in Yosemite.

Erik wasn't the first person ever to scale El Capitan. But he was the first blind person to do it. Erik was born with a rare, degenerative eye disease and was completely blind by age thirteen, sightless before he accomplished any of these feats. But Erik will tell you blindness isn't a disability. It's only a nuisance. It doesn't mean you can't do things. It just means you have to find different ways of doing them.

A disability is in the body.

A handicap is in the mind.

Too many of us make the mistake of not distinguishing one from the other.

> *I can do everything with the help of Christ who gives me the strength I need.*
>
> PHILIPPIANS 4:13 NLT

Good News About Difficulties

I discovered a fifteen-word sentence this week which contains one of life's most important insights: "Life is hard and when we come to terms with that, it no longer matters."

Of course life is hard. We may face different difficulties at various stages in our lives, but life is never without challenge.

The newborn baby enters its strange new world with flailing arms, struggling for that first breath of air, and throughout its life the hard work of survival is never done.

As we grow older, we begin to understand. A senior citizen said to her friend, "You know, I survived World War II, three auto accidents, two bad marriages, two depressions, a dozen company strikes, three mortgages, and a bankruptcy. And some fresh teenager has the nerve to tell me, 'You don't know what life is all about.'"

Once we accept that life is difficult, we can forge both happiness and success out of the struggle. But if we demand that life be easy, we're destined to discover neither happiness nor success.

Consider it pure joy, my brothers, whenever you face trials of many kinds, because you know that the testing of your faith develops perseverance. Perseverance must finish its work so that you may be mature and complete, not lacking anything.

JAMES 1:2-4 NIV

Learning From Their Mistakes

> *Failure is only an opportunity to begin again more intelligently.*
>
> —HENRY FORD

There's a Chinese proverb that says: "If you wish to be successful, talk to three old men."

And, recently, an American research organization talked to several hundred men over the age of sixty and asked them to list their biggest mistakes. Several regrets turned up again and again. They were:

1. dropping out of college.
2. failing to stick with anything.
3. failing to save money.
4. refusing a steady job with a good firm.
5. rejecting the advice of older, wiser heads.
6. playing it safe and missing the big opportunity.
7. failing to work hard enough.

These were the seven major regrets of most older men surveyed regardless of profession or income.

Learning from the mistakes of others is the easiest way to prevent some of our own. Especially the kinds of mistakes that can't ever be corrected.

He who heeds instruction is on the path to life, but he who rejects reproof goes astray.

PROVERBS 10:17 RSV

The Joy of a Good Mistake

> *He who has never failed somewhere, that man cannot be great.*
>
> —HERMAN MELVILLE
>
> *To make no mistake is not in the power of man; but from their errors and mistakes the wise and good learn wisdom for the future.*
>
> —PLUTARCH

*T*here are two kinds of mistakes: Those that teach. And those that destroy. That second kind we certainly want to avoid. But the first kind, the teaching kind, not only are okay, they're necessary.

When I began flight training, my instructor allowed me to make mistakes. Even encouraged it. But within limits. He was careful to see that I didn't do something from which the airplane couldn't recover.

Too often we go through life afraid to make mistakes. But there's no progress, no growth without them. What matters is that we distinguish between mistakes from which we can recover and those which might be fatal.

I heard a prominent publisher say recently that out of the past twenty-one years he'd had only one really bad year. And that year, he said, taught him a lot. Mostly it taught him how to never have another year like that.

The best mistakes are the ones that not only are survivable, but that also empower us to not make them again. And attempting to avoid *all* mistakes would be the biggest mistake of all.

> *This is what the Lord says: When people fall down, don't they get up again? When they start down the wrong road and discover their mistake, don't they turn back?*
>
> JEREMIAH 8:4 NLT

An Audience of One

> Have you had a kindness shown? Pass it on!
> 'Twas not given for thee alone. Pass it on!
> Let it travel down the years.
> Let it wipe another's tears.
> Till in Heaven the deed appears—Pass it on!
> —HENRY BURTON

*T*he size of the audience does not count. It may be a cheering crowd of thousands at a rock concert. Or millions of viewers watching the president on television. Or the audience could be just one person sitting across a candlelit dinner table looking into the loving eyes of someone special.

Clearly, the size of an audience has little to do with its value. As a broadcaster, my words have been heard by countless radio listeners around the world. But was any mass audience ever as important to me as that audience of one little boy and one little girl who years ago sat on my lap to hear bedtime stories?

Aren't you turned off by the arrogant athlete who loves the roar of the crowd but is too busy to give one eager child an autograph? Or the performer who treats individual fans with contempt, apparently forgetting who was responsible for his or her stardom?

Then there was Marian Anderson. After a concert at a small college in Nebraska, the great contralto returned to her hotel. The girl at the desk, working her way through college, told Ms. Anderson how disappointed she was that she'd been unable to attend the performance. Marian Anderson stepped back from the counter, and there, in the hotel lobby, without accompaniment, sang for that audience of one the inspiring *Ave Maria*.

> *Just as you did it to one of the least of these who are members of my family, you did it to me.*
>
> MATTHEW 25:40 NRSV

Good News About Volunteering

> *In the time we have it is surely our duty to do all the good we can to all the people we can in all the ways we can.*
>
> —WILLIAM BARCLAY

They say good news travels slowly. It also travels quietly, so quietly that sometimes we miss it. One of the best stories of our time is one you rarely hear and almost never see in a headline. It's the story of America's volunteers—that mighty army of dedicated citizens who quietly and without fanfare feed the hungry, care for the sick and dying, comfort the lonely, mentor our youth, help the poor, and perform other private acts of mercy we may not even have thought about.

How large is this army? Ninety-three million strong. Nearly half of all Americans volunteer. Each one averages slightly more than four hours a week or half a day's work. And think about this: More than half of our teenagers—60 percent— have enlisted in this army of volunteers.

Next time you pick up your morning paper and read about some heinous crime or some corrupt politician, reflect on the magnificent, largely untold story of these committed citizens. Their work doesn't show up in our gross national product. But if it did, it would add more than two hundred billion dollars.

Half the people in America keep alive the spirit of neighbor helping neighbor by volunteering every week. I wonder what would happen to our country if the other half of us signed up?

> *If you really fulfill the royal law, according to the scripture, "You shall love your neighbor as yourself," you do well.*
>
> JAMES 2:8 RSV

The Joy of Receiving Help

> It is a pleasant thought that when you help a fellow up a steep hill, you get nearer to the top yourself.
>
> —REYNOLDS PRICE

*W*e might be surprised how many resources we have that we don't recognize. Only when we're backed against the wall or kicked to the ground do we start to understand how much help is available.

I arrived at my first Air Force assignment destitute and desperate. Recently married, my wife and I had lost the mobile home we were pulling in an accident. We weren't hurt, but the trailer was totaled. Off-base housing was scarce. What existed was expensive. The accident had left us broke.

We didn't want to worry our parents on the other side of the continent, so we looked for other resources. And we found them: A sympathetic commanding officer who loaned us $20. An understanding schoolteacher and his wife who allowed us to live temporarily in their converted garage. A sergeant who worked on our old clunker of a car to get it running again.

After watching his small son try unsuccessfully to move a heavy rock, the father said, "Son, are you sure you're using *all* your strength?"

"Yes, I am," the boy cried, clearly exasperated

"No, you're not," the father replied, calmly. "You haven't asked *me* to help you."

We'll never know how many hands are willing to help until we reach for them. Nor how much assistance we didn't get simply because we wouldn't ask.

> *Bear one another's burdens, and so fulfil the law of Christ.*
>
> GALATIANS 6:2 RSV

Good News About Kindness

> *What do we live for if not to make life less difficult for each other?*
>
> —GEORGE ELIOT

*A*ssaults against children and older people inevitably make news. And they should. What crime is more despicable than one committed against those vulnerable ones who are least able to defend themselves?

But when someone helps a child or a senior, it rarely gets reported.

Like this story of a younger woman standing in line to pick up a prescription. She was hoping what she did wouldn't be noticed by the elderly woman ahead of her.

The older woman had come up a few cents short of what she owed for her medicine. She seemed confused, searching her purse again and again, trying to find some pennies. Finally the younger woman behind her caught the clerk's eye and, silently, slipped a nickel out of her own purse and onto the counter. With an understanding wink, the clerk turned to the older customer and said, "Oh, here's a nickel." She then completed the sale and the older woman walked away, smiling and without embarrassment.

Three people experienced a moment of happiness that day. And it had cost only a nickel.

You can't always measure the size of a person's generosity by the size of the gift. Sometimes the smallest act of kindness can make the biggest difference.

> *Make love your aim.*
>
> 1 CORINTHIANS 14:1 RSV

One at a Time

> *Get in front of the ball, you won't get hurt. That's what you've got a chest for, young man.*
>
> —JOHN MCGRAW
>
> *The great virtue in life is real courage that knows how to face the facts and live beyond them.*
>
> —D.H. LAWRENCE

When problems overwhelm us and sadness smothers us, where do we find the will and the courage to continue? The answer may come in the caring voice of a friend, a chance encounter with a book, or from personal faith. For Janet, help came from her faith—and from a squirrel.

Shortly after her divorce, Janet lost her father. Then her job. She had mounting money problems.

But Janet not only survived, she worked her way out of despondency, and now life is good again. How? She told me that one late autumn day when she was at her lowest, she watched a squirrel storing up nuts for the winter. One at a time he would take them to the nest. She thought, "If that squirrel can take care of himself, so can I."

"Once I broke my problems into small pieces, I was able to carry them one at a time."

When there's a two-ton boulder between you and happiness, try breaking it up. Boulders are much easier to move one small rock at a time.

Your heavenly Father already knows your needs, and he will give you all you need from day to day if you live for him and make the Kingdom of God your primary concern. So don't worry about tomorrow; for tomorrow will bring its own worries. Today's trouble is enough for today.

MATTHEW 6:32-34 NLT

Finding Joy in the Valleys

> *Character cannot be developed in ease and quiet. Only through experience of trial and suffering can the soul be strengthened, vision cleared, ambition inspired, and success achieved.*
>
> —HELEN KELLER

So, how's life?" I asked my friend. He'd joined me for dinner while I was in his city on business. It was our first meeting since he'd taken the new job and moved away.

"Well, personally, life's great," he said. "But professionally, it could be better."

He then explained how the job he'd been promised when he joined the firm several months earlier finally had opened up, but it was given to someone else. Initially, my friend had been devastated.

"But you know," he said, "my health is good, my wife loves me, we both like our new home, and I'm actually enjoying the job I do have."

That seemed like an unusually positive attitude for someone who'd just had a career door slammed in his face. How did he remain so upbeat?

"It's something my grandmother taught me," he said. "She pointed out that while the view is great from a mountaintop, that's not where things grow. Up there where the snow and the rocks are, you don't see anything green. You have to go down below the timberline.

"And," he continued, "if you really want to go where things bloom best, you have to descend all the way into the valleys."

The mountaintops in life are more fun, but the valleys may be more productive. It's in the low places that things—and people—grow best.

> *Even though I walk through the valley of the shadow of death,*
> *I will fear no evil, for you are with me;*
> *Your rod and your staff, they comfort me.*
>
> PSALM 23:4 NIV

The Joy of Simplicity

Simplicity and clarity—these are the attributes that give our lives power and vividness and joy.

—RICHARD HALLOWAY

*D*o you get the feeling that maybe we're working too hard at having fun?

A friend of mine who is not into opera reluctantly agreed to join his wife for a performance of *Rigoletto*. Only half jokingly, he told me, "I'm planning to enjoy this opera—if it kills me." How many things do we do in the name of enjoyment that really don't bring us much pleasure?

When a favorite aunt invited her five-year-old nephew to spend a day with her, she had everything planned to the last detail. And she had the schedule packed tight. First a morning trip to the amusement park. Then a visit to the circus during the afternoon. Finally a rather elaborate dinner in a fancy restaurant. By the time she dropped the little boy off at his house, the child was exhausted. He told his mom, "Wow, if I'd known what a wonderful day it was going to be, I'd have stayed home."

When I see grown-ups trying too hard to have fun, I wonder why they don't just ease up. Back off. Go with the flow. It was Henry Thoreau who warned that our lives are frittered away in detail. His advice: Simplify. Simplify. When fun becomes work, it stops being fun. When we overcomplicate happiness, we lose it.

It is in the simple things all around us that we may find our greatest pleasure—provided we're not too busy to notice them.

> Wisdom has built her spacious house with seven pillars. She has prepared a great banquet, mixed the wines, set the table. She has sent her servants to invite everyone to come.... "Come home with me," she urges the simple. To those without good judgment, she says, "Come eat my food, and drink the wine I have mixed. Leave your foolish ways behind, and begin to live; learn how to be wise."
>
> WISDOM 9:1-6 NLT

Follow a Leader

> *People seldom improve when they have no other model but themselves to copy.*
>
> —OLIVER GOLDSMITH

*T*here was a time when I had difficulty getting and staying on a regular exercise routine. So I engaged a personal trainer three days a week to set the pace for my workouts. Because I was paying the trainer, it was somehow easier to stay with the schedule, even on days when I didn't particularly feel like it.

All of us need pacesetters in our lives. People who can make us work a little harder. Stretch a little more. Push on a little farther. It's how we grow.

Of course we don't always like it. When Tom D. was in army basic training at Fort Leonard Wood, Missouri, his drill sergeant one morning announced that he had good news and bad news. He said the good news was that Private Buford would be setting the pace for the morning run. Now the troops did consider that good news because Private Buford was overweight and known to be terribly slow.

The bad news? Oh, the drill sergeant said, the bad news is that Private Buford will be driving a truck.

To make progress in life, set your sights on the person who

has already arrived at the place you want to be. The only pace-setter worth following is the one in front of you.

> *Follow my example, as I follow the example of Christ.*
>
> 1 CORINTHIANS 11:1 NIV

The Joy of Silence

> *Silence is as full of potential wisdom and wit as the unhewn marble of great sculpture.*
>
> —ALDOUS HUXLEY

*R*ecently my wife and I journeyed to a tiny tropical island to write a book. Only five people live permanently on the island. There's one cellular phone and one television set. It sits above the outdoor bar at the island's only restaurant.

The island is a lush, green place devoid of distraction. A perfect setting for an author. Writing requires less discipline when there's nothing else to do. But at night, this tiny Caribbean paradise provides an unanticipated bonus. After the last visiting boat engine is shut down, the last light extinguished, and the last radio turned off, the island envelops its visitors with an eerie absence of sound. Silence. Absolute, breathtaking silence.

For a broadcaster from the big city, silence so awesome can be disconcerting. But it grows on you. And for the first time in a long time, you find you actually can hear *yourself.* Your own *thoughts.* Your anxieties and aspirations. Your fears and dreams.

In the silence, the *how-to's* of life are dwarfed by the *what for!*

If you haven't tried total silence lately, I heartily recommend it. You may discover, as I did, it's the most majestic sound you'll *never* hear.

> *Be still, and know that I am God!*
>
> PSALM 46:10 NRSV

Self-Exams

> *He that would well and correctly judge his own faults should not so rigorously judge the faults of his neighbor.*
>
> —THOMAS À KEMPIS

*E*ver notice how the fault we see in some-body else often reflects the same weakness in ourselves?

I knew a woman who was obsessed with her hair. Never liked the way it looked. Interestingly, she also was critical of the hairstyle worn by every woman she saw. And a man with whom I once did business had *zero* tolerance for anyone with a domineering personality. You guessed it. This man was one of the most dictatorial, demanding people you would ever meet.

Maybe it's easier to see someone else's defects and overlook our own because we spend so much more time looking out than we do looking in. The spinach on the other guy's teeth is more obvious to us than the gravy stain on our own necktie.

Of course it's not only easier to see the faults of others, it's more satisfying.

When a professor at the University of Kentucky quit smoking, she was told it would leave her nervous and irritable. She'd been a two-to-three-packs-a-day person for years.

However, the professor says it didn't happen. She says, "I stayed my old sweet self. But my friends got so disagreeable I couldn't stand them."

There would be twice as much progress in the world if we spent half as much time trying to improve ourselves as we do trying to improve others.

> Why do you see the speck in your neighbor's eye, but do not notice the log in your own eye?... First take the log out of your own eye, and then you will see clearly to take the speck out of your neighbor's eye.
>
> LUKE 6:41-42 NRSV

Healing Help

> *Adversity causes some men to break, others to break records.*
>
> —WILLIAM A. WARD

*G*eorge lived by his strong, skilled hands. His entire career depended upon them.

Then suddenly one day, with one crushing blow, George lost his hands and most of his forearms in a forklift accident. Metal hooks replaced the hands that once held his tools and his children.

Such a tragedy might have meant the end. But for this determined Baltimore man, it signaled a new beginning. He *would* be a carpenter again. He *would* pick up a hammer again.

With the help of three students from Johns Hopkins University, George is doing all those things. Jay, one of the students, lost both his legs to a land mine during the Gulf War. Jay has overcome his calamity and now walks so well with artificial legs that there's barely a limp.

So Jay and two other engineering students helped design special tools for George. And a special toolbox. What George still lacks in dexterity, he's making up for with patience. He is becoming a carpenter again. One colleague says that he's awesome. George says just wait. This is only the beginning. The new beginning!

> *The Lord is near to the brokenhearted,*
> *and saves the crushed in spirit.*
> *Many are the afflictions of the righteous;*
> *but the Lord delivers him out of them all.*
>
> PSALM 34:18-19 RSV

The Joy of Serving

The service we render to others is really the rent we pay for our room on this earth.

—WILFRED GRENFELL

*E*ven the toughest of the tough guys occasionally shows a soft spot.

Two Catholic nuns knew there were lots of tough guys in the neighborhood where their car had stalled. They hoped they could get out of there before someone came over to make trouble for them. As they bowed their heads, praying for some sort of mechanical miracle, one especially menacing looking man stomped over to their car and tapped on the window. He motioned for the sisters to get out.

With great apprehension, but feeling they had little choice, the two women obeyed. The man turned the key in the ignition, then pulled the hood latch. He poked around the battery for a few minutes, moving a few wires around. Then, he climbed behind the wheel and the car started for him immediately.

The nuns were overjoyed. How could they thank this unlikely angel? Could they pay him something for his trouble? The tough guy, looking more like a thug than a good Samaritan, simply shrugged and said, "That's all right, ladies.

I ain't never been the answer to a prayer before."

Nothing does us more good than doing good for someone else. And if there's anything more gratifying than having a prayer answered, it's discovering we are the answer.

> *For who is greater, the one who is at the table or the one who serves? Is it not the one who is at the table? But I am among you as one who serves.*
>
> LUKE 22:27 NIV

When Knowledge Is Power

> Why always "not yet"? Do flowers in spring say "not yet"?
>
> —NORMAN DOUGLAS

*W*e've all laughed at the auto mechanic whose own car never seems to run right. Or the TV repairman, so busy fixing everyone else's set, his own is on the blink. It's not unusual to leave jobs undone, even though we possess the expertise to do them. There certainly are men and women with knowledge enough to be excellent parents, but with lives so busy they simply don't take the time to apply what they know. And ministers' wives commonly complain that their husbands are so busy counseling and caring for other families they often neglect their own.

When University of Illinois professor John Bardeen won the Nobel physics prize for developing transistors, he was late for the press conference because the garage door on his house got stuck. The garage door that worked on a transistorized circuit. Knowing how to do something is not the same as doing it, and expertise that isn't exercised is as useless as if it didn't exist.

The old challenge, "Physician, heal thyself," applies to all of us. We've been told that knowledge is power. But knowledge is not power until it's applied.

> *Listen to the words of the wise; apply your heart to my instruction. For it is good to keep these sayings deep within yourself, always ready on your lips.*
>
> PROVERBS 22:17 NLT

Roots

*H*istory teaches. It also humbles. Any study of the past reveals how dependent everything we do is upon what others already have done. A case in point: Today's dramatic space exploration is built upon basic scientific principles discovered decades ago—some of them, centuries ago.

Take the computer: Did you know that the origins of this high tech device can be traced to a *woman* in the 1800s? Ada Byron was the daughter of Lord Byron, a gifted, but slightly crazy poet. Five weeks after Ada was born, her mother left the eccentric poet.

Terrified that Ada might have inherited her dad's poetic genes, Lady Byron brought up her daughter to be a mathematician and scientist. At the age of nineteen, Ada heard about a new "calculating engine" developed by a scientist named Babbage. She began corresponding with Babbage, eventually convincing him there was a way his new engine could calculate Bernoulli numbers.

Now I'm not a mathematician, so don't ask me what Bernoulli numbers are. All I know is that Daniel Bernoulli developed a mathematical equation so important that today Ada Byron's plan is regarded as the world's first computer program. In fact, the U.S. Defense Department once named a software program Ada in her honor.

Even if we're standing on our own two feet, those feet are planted firmly on the shoulders of those whose names we don't even know.

> *At many moments in the past and by many means, God spoke to our ancestors through the prophets; but in our time, the final days, he has spoken to us in the person of his Son, whom he appointed heir of all things and through whom he made the ages.*
>
> HEBREWS 1:1-2 NJB

The Joy of Truthfulness

> Make yourself an honest man and then you
> may be sure there is one rascal less in the
> world.
>
> —THOMAS CARLYLE

When our son was a teenager seeking his first regular summer job, the application asked for previous work experience. Al put down everything he could think of from mowing lawns to carrying out trash to helping a neighbor build a toolshed. Some of his descriptions seemed a bit long on embellishment.

But such is the insecurity of youth, embarrassed by a lack of formal job experience.

After one young man's friends advised him to exaggerate his work record while being interviewed for a first job, he was all prepared to fake it. As he waited in the lobby for the personnel director, a pleasant young woman, apparently a secretary, sat down and began asking him about his interests, his hobbies, his ambitions. For nearly an hour he candidly and enthusiastically answered each question.

Finally, when he inquired as to how soon he might expect the job interview, she replied, "This was it. I'm the personnel director. I like your sincerity and your honesty. You've got the job."

Most employers would rather hire a truthful novice than an experienced exaggerator. Honesty *is* the best policy. In résumés, and in life.

> *Listen, for I have worthy things to say;*
> *I open my lips to speak what is right.*
> *My mouth speaks what is true,*
> *for my lips detest wickedness.*
>
> PROVERBS 8:6-8 NIV

The Mark of a Child

> *The more opinions you have, the less you see.*
> —WIM WENDERS

My regular morning exercise routine is a brisk walk along the lake, only this time I'd decided to take a different route and turn the walk into a trip to the neighborhood hardware store. A stretch of new sidewalk had been installed since my last trek down that street. And right in the middle of one freshly poured rectangle of concrete was a crudely drawn face and two initials—obviously the work of some child.

My reaction was instantaneous: How dare that inconsiderate youngster mess up a perfectly troweled piece of concrete? This little boy or girl had defaced a part of my neighborhood and I'd have to look at this ugly, inlaid graffiti for years to come.

But then I had a second thought: Neighborhoods aren't about smooth concrete and perfect sidewalks and manicured lawns. They're about moms and dads and kids. They're about families. Perhaps instead of being a symbol of vandalism, this childish imprint was a monument to proper priorities.

I got a lot out of my walk that morning. Fresh air. Good

exercise. And a reminder etched in concrete that children are more important than sidewalks.

> *He called a little child to him whom he set among them. Then he said, "In truth I tell you, unless you change and become like little children you will never enter the kingdom of Heaven. And so, the one who makes himself as little as this little child is the greatest in the kingdom of Heaven."*
>
> MATTHEW 18:2-4 NJB

The Joy of Work

> *Sweat plus sacrifice equals success.*
> —CHARLES O. FINLEY

When the cocky young player said he knew that their team would take the pennant because they had the will to win, his manager said, "Don't kid yourself. The will to win isn't worth a darn without the will to prepare!"

Just about everybody wants to succeed. But not everybody is willing to do what it takes to succeed: to apply the self-discipline, the hard work that leads to professionalism.

After Jack Valenti lectured college students about the movie business, a twenty-one-year-old film major complained that the Hollywood establishment had shut him out. Valenti asked about the young man's experience in filmmaking. Well, it consisted of an eight-millimeter documentary he'd once shot about his college basketball team. Did he have any scripts ready for someone in Hollywood to shoot? No, but he had seen a lot of movies and he had some good ideas. As the late Harry Blackstone once said about being a magician, "There's nothing I do that can't be done by a ten-year-old—with fifteen years of practice."

For all the dramatic changes we've seen in the workplace, the formula for success remains what it has always been: dedication and hard work. So far, no one has come up with a better one.

> Idler, go to the ant;
>   ponder her ways and grow wise....
> All through the summer she gets her food ready, and gathers her supplies at harvest time.
>
> PROVERBS 6:6, 8 NJB

Follow Through

> *Either do not attempt at all, or go through with it.*
>
> —OVID

*T*alk is easy. Walking the talk can be hard. Joe Griffith was browsing through a sporting goods store when he overheard this discussion between a father and his teenage son.

"Please, Dad, if you buy me the weight set, I'll lift them every day. I promise."

"Well, son, I don't know ..."

"C'mon, Dad, I promise. Just buy them for me and I promise I'll use them."

"Oh, all right. If you're really going to take the training seriously. If you'll make good use of them, I'll buy the weights." The father paid for the equipment and started walking toward the door.

Moments later Joe heard the son's voice calling after the father, "What? You mean I gotta carry them out to the car?"

A promise is like the swing of a baseball bat or a golf club. No matter how good it is, it's not good enough unless we've learned to follow through. Following through is something winners in sports and in life all know how to do.

The truly wise never believe a word is sufficient. They know that an ounce of action is worth a pound of talk.

> *A man had two sons; and he went to the first and said, "Son, go and work in the vineyard today." And he answered, "I will not"; but afterward he repented and went. And he went to the second and said the same; and he answered, "I go, sir," but did not go. Which of the two did the will of his father?*
>
> MATTHEW 21:28-31 RSV

Good News About Service

A writer for *Sports Illustrated* once wrote this envious note about a Kentucky Derby winner: "He's everything that I am not. He is young; he is beautiful; he has lots of hair; he is fast; he is durable; he has a large bank account; and his entire sex life is before him." There's nothing wrong with money, security, power, and sex appeal. Few of us would refuse them.

But the playboy type for whom these become primary goals in life ultimately discovers their promise of satisfaction and fulfillment is an illusion. Those whose circle of concern isn't wide enough to take in other people inevitably end up disappointed and usually bitter. Money, power, security, and sex appeal provide certain rewards, but a happy and contented life isn't one of them.

The sense of well-being all of us crave comes only from understanding the great paradox of life: That the more we give, the more we get. From the highest paid executive to the most modestly compensated worker, the secret to inner peace is the same. Service expands our capacity to enjoy life. Selfishness contracts it.

Life is a lot like tennis. The winners usually are those who've learned to serve the best.

> *Whoever wants to be first must be last of all and servant of all.*
>
> MARK 9:35 NRSV

Celebrate the Difference

Female and male God made the man, His image is the whole, not half.
—COVENTRY PATMORE

*H*ow much difference between girls and boys is learned, how much genetic? That's still being debated. Judy recalls a birthday party where her daughter received a small doll stroller. She promptly put one of her new dolls in it and started to push it around. A little boy at the party just as promptly turned it over and tried to pull the wheels off.

Personality differences between male and female also are observable in animals and sometimes seem strangely familiar: Scientists studying gorillas note that the largest and most vocal male gorilla always appears to be in charge. But closer observation shows something else: Even as the male stomps around, making lots of noise and pretending to call the shots, he's actually looking over his shoulder for cues from the group's real decision makers—the females.

If the females show disapproval, the male will suddenly inspect his fingernails or start scratching an imaginary flea while he reorganizes his thoughts and figures out how to do what the females want—without losing face. He wants credit for having thought up the plan himself, while making sure the females get what *they* want out of the deal.

I don't know—makes you think the gorillas have been observing us! Sounds to me like a clear case of monkey see, monkey do. Sometimes it's healthier to appreciate our differences and learn to laugh at them than it is to eliminate them. It's also easier.

> *So God created man in his own image, in the image of God he created him; male and female he created them.*
>
> GENESIS 1:27 RSV

The Right Idea About Violence

> *The wish to hurt, the momentary intoxication with pain, is the loophole through which the pervert climbs into the minds of ordinary men.*
>
> —JACOB BRONOWSKI

A few years ago a couple of our state legislators made headlines by getting into a fistfight while debating a bill. I also recall seeing a report from Taiwan where it appeared the entire legislative body had gotten into a free-for-all with fists swinging and papers flying.

The Chinese tell a story about two peasants, arguing heatedly when a stranger walks by. Observing the intensity of their anger, he says that he is surprised that they haven't come to blows. Then his Chinese friend explains, "The man who strikes first admits that his ideas have given out."

Violence usually means someone's ideas have given out. Dictators keep their people in line with guns because the ideas behind their regimes aren't strong enough.

Once I heard about a small boy who got into an argument with boys twice his size, then drew a line in the dirt and dared them to cross it. They thought he was crazy. But when the first boy stepped across, the little guy said, "Okay, now you're on *my* side." I think you'll agree that this lad had found the right idea.

> *If anyone hits you on the right cheek, offer him the other as well.*
>
> MATTHEW 5:39 NJB

What Makes Us Happy

> *The U.S. Constitution doesn't guarantee happiness, only the pursuit of it. You have to catch up with it yourself.*
>
> —BENJAMIN FRANKLIN

*R*ecently, Duke University's Sociology Department set out to discover what makes people happy. They came up with nine principles, and while none is a *new* concept, all are worth reviewing:

1. People who are happy are not suspicious or resentful and they don't carry grudges.

2. They live in the present and aren't preoccupied with past failures and mistakes.

3. They don't waste time.

4. They cooperate with life.

5. Happy people force themselves to be outgoing with others.

6. They don't pity themselves or make excuses for their mistakes.

7. Happy people cultivate the traditional virtues of love, honor, loyalty, and thrift.

8. They set realistic goals.

9. Happy people believe in something bigger than them-selves. And for most, that's faith in God.

The secret to happiness isn't a secret at all. It's a set of proven principles known since ancient times. The only thing mysterious about happiness is why more people don't figure it out.

> *This is the day which the Lord has made;*
> *let us rejoice and be glad in it.*
>
> PSALM 118:24 RSV

The Joy of Discretion

A talented but rather reserved executive I once knew explained why he seldom spoke out at meetings: "I'd rather keep my mouth shut and have people suspect I'm ignorant," he would say, "than to open my mouth and have them convinced of it."

The man was joking, of course. He was anything but ignorant. But there was considerable wisdom in his quip. Because the smartest and sharpest people in the world always spend more time listening than they do talking. That way there's always more going into their brains than coming out.

Not like the baseball manager who had authored three autobiographies. A friend noted he was the only guy who had written more books than he had read. We respect people who listen more than they talk because when they do speak, it's likely to be important.

A wise statement is measured by its depth, not its length. The strongest ideas require the fewest words. Some need no words at all.

> Be attentive to my wisdom, incline your ear to
>   my understanding;
> that you may keep discretion, and your lips
>   may guard knowledge.
>
> PROVERBS 5:1-2 RSV

Listen Up

> The most important thing in communication
> is to hear what isn't being said.
>
> —PETER DRUCKER

*O*ften after I've delivered a speech I'm asked to engage in a question-and-answer session. I usually joke with the audience that I have plenty of answers. I only hope the answers match their questions.

How many times we've all answered questions that weren't being asked. Like the question of the five-year-old who asked, "Daddy, where did I come from?" After the father nervously completed a rather detailed explanation about reproduction, the boy said, "No, Daddy, I mean where did I *come* from like Jimmy? Jimmy says he came from Cleveland."

Carol Burnett once had a serious heart-to-heart talk with her seven-year-old daughter, Carrie, as she was putting the little girl to bed. She discussed love and character and why it was important always to do the right thing. The child was so serious and attentive, studying Carol's face so intently that Carol was starting to congratulate herself on really getting through. Then Carrie looked her mom in the eye and said, "Mommy, how many teeth do you have?"

The reason some people have all the answers is because they haven't heard all the questions.

> *Happy is the man who listens to me*
> *[wisdom], watching daily at my gates,*
> *waiting beside my doors.*
> *For he who finds me finds life and obtains*
> *favor from the Lord.*
>
> PROVERBS 8:34-35 RSV

The Joy of Overcoming Weaknesses

> *Life affords no higher pleasure than that of surmounting difficulties.*
>
> —SAMUEL JOHNSON

Some of the best things I've done were things I didn't want to do, but went ahead and did anyway. For example, a few years ago my doctor got me into a physical fitness program which, honestly, I didn't want to do. But as my weight and blood pressure dropped and I generally began feeling better, I was glad I'd done something I didn't want to do.

As a child I was quite shy. Introverted. Embarrassed around people. I forced myself to audition for school plays and to take a speech course. By doing what I didn't want to do, I gained confidence and an ability to easily meet and interact with people.

A woman I know hated reading. But when her children came along she realized she ought to read to them. So she forced herself to take a literature class. That got her so hooked on books that now she thoroughly enjoys them.

After listening to a talented tenor belt out a rousing pop song at one of those karaoke places, I asked him how he'd developed such an exceptional voice.

"As a kid, I hated singing," he explained. "Didn't think I could carry a tune. So I forced myself to do it. Now I love it."

There can be great benefit in doing what we don't want to do. Sometimes our greatest strength is that weakness we'd do anything to hide. So stop hiding it.

> He said to me, "My grace is sufficient for you, for my power is made perfect in weakness." I will all the more gladly boast of my weaknesses, that the power of Christ may rest upon me.... for when I am weak, then I am strong.
>
> 2 CORINTHIANS 12:9-10 RSV

Greed Is for the Birds

People who live for self never succeed in satisfying self or anybody else.

—CHARLES G. TRUMBULL

*T*he ducks clearly were accustomed to boats coming in and out of the harbor. And it was just as clear they were used to being fed by the boaters. No sooner had Renee and I tied up than at least a dozen ducks paddled up to our stern, quacking, splashing, and making it quite obvious they expected something from the new arrivals.

Renee brought some bread up on deck. We pulled it into several pieces and tossed them all into the water. And a funny thing happened. Five of the ducks clustered around one small piece of bread and began fighting for it. All around them lay other chunks of bread, several larger than the tidbit for which these daffy ducks were competing. Eventually we dropped whole slices of bread onto the water but it didn't matter. Inevitably, three, four, or five ducks would home in on a single crumb and began squabbling over it.

Sometimes we humans aren't that much different. We may grumble about somebody else's success or resent that slice of the pie our neighbor or our competitor is getting. Meanwhile, we aren't recognizing the bigger slices all around us for the taking.

Those ducks could have had plenty of bread without a single fight. All they needed was more vision and less greed.

Pulling ourselves up doesn't mean we have to pull other people down. It isn't necessary to take theirs in order to find ours.

> *So always treat others as you would like them to treat you; that is the Law and the Prophets.*
>
> MATTHEW 7:12 NJB

The Joy of Self-Knowledge

> *I am somebody. I am me. I like being me. And*
> *I need nobody to make me somebody.*
>
> —LOUIS L'AMOUR

Several years ago, when I was anchoring television news, a young woman approached me in a shopping mall. She knew the face but couldn't place the name. Finally she asked, "Hey, aren't you somebody?" I knew what she meant. Aren't you somebody I should know? Aren't you somebody I've seen on television? But the way she put the question got me to thinking about how we categorize people. Famous. Rich. Important. Very important. *Un*important.

Who can ever forget the unfortunate comment attributed to a wealthy New York hotel owner? Accused of cheating on her taxes, she's alleged to have said, "Only little people pay taxes."

Well, if there are any little people in the world it's people with that kind of attitude. People with small spirits. Narrow minds. The biggest people recognize that there really are no little people. Everybody is somebody and everybody is important. When a new employee told radio station owner Lloyd Johnson of Ann Arbor, Michigan, "You must have met a lot of very important people in your lifetime," Johnson replied, "I never met one who wasn't."

If you want to be a VIP, start by recognizing that you already are one. When you believe in your own worth, others will eventually get the idea.

> At that time, the disciples came to Jesus and asked, "Who is the greatest in the kingdom of heaven?" He called a little child and had him stand among them. And he said: "... whoever humbles himself like this child is the greatest in the kingdom of heaven."
>
> MATTHEW 18:1-2, 4 NIV

Healthful Friendships

> Friends are the sunshine of life.
>
> —JOHN HAY

*O*ccasionally a scientific study produces results that seem to make little sense. Take one conducted by psychologist Sheldon Cohen at Carnegie-Mellon University. He discovered that people who spend lots of time alone contract more colds than those who are socially active.

Now since colds result from germs being passed around, isn't it logical that the most socially active would come down with the most colds? Yet in Cohen's study, fewer than half of those with good friends and close family ties got sick while nearly two-thirds of those without good relationships fell victim to cold germs.

Dr. Cohen himself admits he's a bit baffled by the results. Is it just possible that people who like people have better immune systems? That a healthy interest in others makes for a healthier you? After all, there are those other studies showing that married men live longer than single men. Clearly there's some connection between human connectedness and health. Maybe when it comes to cold remedies, relationships are nothing to sneeze at.

Being socially active may or may not prevent colds. But it couldn't hurt.

And like chicken soup and a good night's sleep, it's bound to make you feel better.

> *He who is a friend is always a friend, and a brother is born for the time of stress.*
>
> PROVERBS 17:17 NAB

The Joy of Kindness

> *Without kindness, there can be no true joy.*
> —THOMAS CARLYLE
>
> *I expect to pass through life but once. If, therefore, there be any kindness I can show, or any good thing I can do for any fellow being, let me do it now... as I shall not pass this way again.*
> —WILLIAM PENN

Shakespeare described the world as a stage and human beings as actors—each of us playing a part. But what kind of stage is it? And what kind of role do we play?

Is it possible that the stage is whatever we choose and the role, whatever we select? Surely we can give some direction to this drama called life.

There was a movie producer-director several years ago named King Vidor. Vidor lived in California but frequently had to visit New York. He always found the cab drivers there impatient and rude. They seemed to detest their jobs and their customers.

One day while in New York, King Vidor stumbled across this quotation by William Makepeace Thackeray: *The world is a looking glass and gives back to every man the reflection of his own face.* Then King Vidor wondered, "Could this situation with the cabbies be partly my fault?" So that day he changed his own attitude. Instead of snarling at the cabbies, he went out of his way to be friendly.

Vidor says *that day* he didn't come across one single taxi driver who was unpleasant. Even convenience store clerks and hotel employees seemed friendlier than he'd ever known them to be.

It doesn't matter whether it's the boss, the clerk, or your mother-in-law. Life is a mirror. And it really does reflect back to us what we put in front of it.

> *Be kind to one another, tenderhearted, forgiving one another, as God in Christ forgave you.*
> EPHESIANS 4:32 RSV

Just Do It

> *Even if you're on the right track, you'll get run over if you just sit there.*
>
> —WILL ROGERS

*C*reating a great set does not a movie make. The movie was being filmed on location in the lobby of our hotel. Preparations had been elaborate and time-consuming. Technicians and creative types had spent days attending to every detail from scenery to lighting to proper placement of microphones.

It occurred to me that for all the money and planning that had gone into creating this movie environment, there wouldn't be a movie until the director gave that crucial one-word order, *Action!*

He could call for lights. Call for the camera to roll. Ask for a sound check. But until he uttered that powerful, six-letter word, *action*, nothing would happen.

Too often we get hung up on the planning part of life and never get around to the action. We spend all our time getting ready to do something, but then we never do it. We're good on the lights, the camera, the scenery, the sound, but we're real slow on the action.

During World War II, when an army engineer told General

Douglas MacArthur it would take three days to construct a river bridge, MacArthur said, "Good. Start drawing up the plans right away."

Sure enough, three days later the bridge was done. When MacArthur asked to see *the plans,* the engineer said, "General, you can send your troops across that bridge right now. But if you want to wait until the plans are done, that'll take quite awhile."

> *Be doers of the word, and not hearers only.*
>
> JAMES 1:22 RSV

Enjoying Solitude

> *To live happily is an inward power of the soul.*
>
> —MARCUS AURELIUS

There used to be a restaurant in my home-town that was a favorite hangout for kids. Usually the jukebox was blaring at full blast, one hit tune after the other. But the restaurant owner recognized that some people did not want music with their meal. So, he wisely had placed in that jukebox a blank recording without a sound on it. For a quarter a customer could purchase three minutes of silence.

I suppose there are times in our noisy world when we'd be willing to pay a lot more than that. Our need to escape the clatter of modern life is why so many of us take drives into the country or seek out the most remote spots we can find for vacations.

It's why some of us try to schedule quiet times on our daily calendars—moments to get in touch with our own thoughts and with God.

It's why playwright George Bernard Shaw once summoned the headwaiter over to his table as the orchestra began to play loudly and asked the waiter, "Does the orchestra play requests?" The waiter was delighted that such a famous person was in his restaurant and he said, "Why, of course, Mr. Shaw. The orchestra would be honored to take your request. What would you like them to play?"

Shaw replied, "Ask them to play dominoes until I've finished eating."

Just as a firefly can best be seen in total darkness, so some of our finest thoughts can only be heard in silence. And solitude can be the best place for us to communicate with God.

> *Search your hearts and be silent.*
>
> PSALM 4:4 NIV

The Joy of Persistence

> *In soloing—as in other activities—it is far easier to start something than it is to finish it.*
>
> —AMELIA EARHART

You'd be amazed to know how many people build and fly their own airplanes. At the Experimental Aircraft Association's annual summer convention, thousands of amateur aircraft makers fly their home-builts to Oshkosh, Wisconsin—some from as far away as Brazil and Australia. Many are truly works of art and may represent years of patient, tedious effort by their owners.

That's why not every pilot who starts to construct an airplane completes it. My aviation magazines regularly carry ads for uncompleted kit plane projects in various stages of assembly.

History also confirms that starting is easier than finishing. Michelangelo created his statue of David—one of the world's great masterpieces—from a block of marble that a previous sculptor had so badly hacked that his backers forced him to abandon the project.

What do you want to create? A healthier body? An improved mind? A more positive outlook? These are all possible if we remember that what enthusiasm starts, commitment has to finish.

Enthusiasm may be the spark that ignites us, but determination is the fuel that keeps us running until we've reached our goal.

> *The one who endures to the end will be saved.*
>
> MARK 13:13 NRSV

Fickle Fame

Then teach me, Heav'n! to scorn the guilty bays,
Drive from my breast the lust of praise,
Unblemished let me live, or die unknown;
O grant an honest fame, or grant me none.
—ALEXANDER POPE

*I*t's easy to envy famous people. The money. The adulation. These may cause us to forget just how transitory and temporary fame can be. Andy Warhol believed everyone is entitled to fifteen minutes of fame. But those who count on it for the long haul usually come up short! The first person ever to go over Niagara Falls in a barrel was a schoolteacher in her sixties who hoped the feat would make her so famous she could fund her retirement with a lecture tour. Yet her fame was so fleeting she lived out her days penniless.

When Jackie Gleason was a young comedian he sneaked out of a boardinghouse at a seaside resort one night because he was too poor to pay his rent. He lowered his suitcase out the window, then sauntered out the front door in his swim trunks as though headed for the beach.

Years later, as a matter of conscience, the now-famous

Gleason returned to the boardinghouse to pay the debt. The woman who ran the place remembered him, but apparently was unaware that Gleason was now a big star. As he walked up to the desk, she gasped in horror, "I thought you had drowned." Even the Great One had to recognize that fame has its limits. The best kind of fame—and the only kind worth having—is the recognition that follows those who do something worthwhile. Fame is much better as a perk than it is as a purpose.

> *His mighty arm does tremendous things! How he scatters the proud and haughty ones! He has taken princes from their thrones and exalted the lowly.*
>
> LUKE 1:51–52 NLT

The Joy of Journaling

> Tomorrow hopes we have learned something from yesterday.
>
> —JOHN WAYNE

*M*y mother had an interesting, but difficult, childhood. Both parents died when she was very young. Her own marriage began during the dark days of the Great Depression.

A few years ago I discovered that mother had documented key events in her life in a journal. She shared some of it with me, allowing me to experience through her own words the happiness and sadness, the dreams realized and the hopes unfulfilled, which have made up the rich fabric of this amazing woman's life.

It made me wish that I had kept a similar written record. For mother's journal not only will provide me and my children with a valuable family history; it already has provided her with a form of therapy—a journey of self-discovery.

She told me getting started was the hardest part, because writing isn't easy, even for the professional. When sportswriter Woody Paige was approached by a woman in a hotel bar who offered to do anything he wanted for a hundred dollars, Woody thought for a moment, then said, "Fine. I'm in room

125. Go up there and write my column for tomorrow."

Each of our lives is a story. Those of us who take the time to document it will leave our children a valuable guide to understanding. We may also learn much about ourselves. So brace yourself and get started.

> *I recall the days of old,*
> *reflecting on all your deeds,*
> *I ponder the works of your hands.*
>
> PSALM 143:5 NJB

To Do or to Be?

Life, we learn too late, is in the living, in the tissue of every day and hour.

—STEPHEN LEACOCK

*I*f you're like most of us you probably have a *to do* list: Fill the car up. Pick up the cleaning. Call the repair person. And so on. Well, I'd like to suggest that you add to your list some things that I think just might help you have a better, more productive day.

Put on that list *daydreaming*. Take time to let your imagination conjure up some new objective or rekindle some long forgotten passion.

Put *hope* on the list. Things probably will get hectic at some point today. Keep hope in focus, knowing that whatever it is, this too shall pass.

I'd also recommend you put *help* on your list. If you get the chance to help someone out today, you'll get even more out of it than they will.

And don't forget *fun*. Whatever else you do today, if you don't have some fun, what's the point?

There was a very cautious man,
Who never laughed or played.
He never risked, he never tried.

He never sang or prayed.
And when he one day passed away,
His insurance was denied.
For since he never really lived,
They claimed he never died!

Maybe it's not enough to carry a list of what we need to do today. Maybe we should also have a list of what we want to be!

> *For everything there is a season, and a time for every matter under heaven: ... a time to weep, and a time to laugh; a time to mourn, and a time to dance; ... a time to embrace, and a time to refrain from embracing; ... a time to keep silence, and a time to speak; ... What gain has the worker from his toil?*
>
> ECCLESIASTES 3:1-9 RSV

Friends or Freud?

> The most called-upon prerequisite of a friend is an accessible ear.
>
> —MAYA ANGELOU
>
> If you want to be listened to, you should put in time listening.
>
> —MARGE PIERCY

*T*he women were discussing their morning over lunch. One had just come from visiting her psychiatrist. "I don't know if this therapy thing is worth all it's costing me," she said. "But it does provide me with someone who'll listen."

It should not diminish the value of psychiatry and psychology to admit that many who seek such counseling don't really need it. What they do need is someone who'll listen. Professionals provide a valuable service to patients who are mentally or emotionally disturbed, and it may be important to seek them out in a crisis situation.

But friends of mine who are in the profession tell me candidly, many of their patients really don't need therapy—they just need someone to listen.

Greek actress Melina Mercouri once made a comment to a

reporter that may have been more profound than she recognized. Melina said, "We don't have psychoanalysis in Greece, you know. We are a poor people, so we have friends instead." The truth is, people who have friends may be broke. But they're never really poor. And those who don't have friends may go broke just trying to pay for all that therapy.

It was Walter Winchell who said, "A real friend is one who walks in when the rest of the world walks out." Sometimes we need to be the friend who's listened to. Sometimes the friend who does the listening.

> No one can have greater love than to lay down his life for his friends.
>
> JOHN 15:13 NJB

The Joy of Human Potential

> *Faith that the thing can be done is essential to any great achievement.*
>
> —THOMAS N. CARRUTHER

*P*redicting a person's potential is riskier than predicting the stock market. If you don't think so, just go back to your high school yearbook and check up on those kids everybody thought were losers. You'll discover some of them became super achievers while a few considered most likely to succeed—didn't.

The New York Opera Newsletter carried a story by Nancy Stokes about a dinner Nancy and her husband, Sherrill, were having with a well-known singing coach. They played a recording of a young, college-age man and asked the coach, "What do you think?"

"Not a chance," the famous voice teacher replied. "Don't encourage him. Tell that guy to get a day job."

Only then did Nancy—whose full name is Nancy Stokes Milnes—reveal that the voice on that tape actually belonged to her husband, one of opera's most accomplished baritones, Sherrill Milnes.

And the voice coach said, "You know, I'll never discourage another young singer again."

Yes, like a stone in the hands of a skilled sculptor or a seed in the care of a good gardener, potential is something that's impossible to see and difficult to predict.

The size of a dream has to be determined by the dreamer. The world is filled with people who, through determination and perseverance, outperformed the limits others had set for them.

> And God blessed them, and God said to them, "Be fruitful and multiply, and fill the earth and subdue it."
>
> GENESIS 1:28 RSV

No Such Luck

> Forget mistakes. Forget failures. Forget every-
> thing except what you're going to do now and
> do it. Today is your lucky day.
>
> —WILL DURANT

A famous physicist had a horseshoe nailed to the wall of his office. A visitor remarked, "Surely a scientist like you doesn't believe in such superstitions." And with a tone of whimsy the physicist replied, "Of course not. But I'm told a horseshoe brings you luck whether you believe in it or not."

The truth is, people who really do believe in luck are the unluckiest people in the world. That's because they sit around waiting for good things to mystically happen, while those who discount the whims of fate are out making things happen. When he was coaching the Miami Dolphins, Don Shula said luck meant a lot in football. And not having a good quarterback was bad luck.

I've never met a truly successful individual whose achievements were based upon luck. In show business, in finance, in politics—those who rise to the top almost invariably create their own lucky breaks by smart planning and hard work.

Unfortunately, too many times we find it easier to hang back and hope than to plunge forward and perform. A psychiatrist says many of his patients discover it's "... easier to lie on a couch digging into the past than it is to sit on a chair facing the present."

It may take even more initiative—and courage—to walk toward the future.

The best way to make this your lucky day is to follow the lead of David Livingstone, the great explorer. He once declared, "I'll go anywhere so long as it is forward."

> *Be careful then how you live, not as unwise people but as wise, making the most of the time.*
>
> EPHESIANS 5:15 NRSV

Gratitude Is Good News

Gratitude is a blessing we give to one another.
—ROBERT RAYNOLDS

*F*ifty years ago Ed Kramer had an idea. A simple idea. Ed believed one of the most important values he could teach his children was gratitude. So he asked them to start looking for the good in people right there in St. Louis where they lived. Every day they were to identify at least three people for whom they could be thankful. A teacher. A friend. Anyone they met.

Each evening at dinnertime they were supposed tell about those people. Then they were to send postcards letting the people know how much they were appreciated. Ed designed special postcards similar to the yellow telegrams of Western Union. He called his card a Thank-U-Gram.

Well, word of this family project spread and people Ed didn't even know began asking for the cards. During the next fifteen years he supplied folks all over America with his Thank-U-Grams. Millions of people including Robert Frost, Leonard Bernstein, Jack Benny, Walt Disney, and even President Eisenhower, asked for these cards.

What began as one man's simple attempt to teach his children mushroomed into a national project of gratitude. When a good idea is unleashed, you just never know where or how far it will go.

We'd be a less cynical society if we took to heart the lesson Ed Kramer taught his children: Look for the good in people. And when you find it let them know.

> *Beloved, if God so loved us, we also ought to love one another.*
>
> 1 JOHN 4:11 RSV

The Joy of Fresh Starts

> *Intelligence is not to make no mistakes, but to quickly see how to make them good.*
>
> —BERTOLT BRECHT

Not so long ago, on a Colorado freeway, I missed my turn and had to travel nearly twenty miles to the next exit. Once the opportunity to make my turn had zipped past, there was no second chance—at least not right away. I was committed.

Some states have recognized that we drivers are human, that we *do* make mistakes. So they've installed turning loops a few hundred feet beyond tricky intersections. These permit drivers to immediately reverse direction.

It's easy on the road of life to nonchalantly speed past opportunities and miss some important turns. It may be the chance to get an education, to change careers, or to initiate a relationship. Occasionally there may be a turnaround allowing an immediate correction. More often, we're committed with no quick fix.

It's not as important *how soon* a second chance comes as it is that we recognize it—*whenever* it comes—and change course.

The longer we head the wrong direction, the longer it'll

take to get back. So look carefully for the next turnaround. And be aware: They aren't always clearly marked. Everyone occasionally takes a wrong turn. But no one has to keep going the wrong direction. The best place to turn around is the first place you see.

> *If someone falls, can he not stand up again?*
> *If people stray, can they not turn back?*
>
> JEREMIAH 8:4 NJB

Good Teachers

Where have all the good teachers gone? If you've ever wondered, then meet Pamela Sue E. At Flanders Elementary she doesn't just introduce her students to geography—she immerses them in it. When they studied the rain forest, the kids raised enough money selling T-shirts to preserve about twenty thousand acres.

At Clarkston Middle School, Ruth D. teaches Shakespeare by encouraging students to debate whether Romeo was guilty or innocent. And she teaches history by having the kids write diary entries as though *they* were the historical figures.

At Hampton Middle School, Virginia B. takes her students to visit senior citizens: to read to them, to write letters for them, and to bring them gifts at holiday time. Virginia believes reading, writing, and arithmetic aren't enough. She's convinced that it's important for youngsters to learn the fourth "R"—*responsibility*.

Throughout this nation there are thousands of teachers

like Pam and Ruth and Virginia. I'll bet you could add some names to the list.

So where have all the good teachers gone? Nowhere.

They're right where they've always been, in the classroom, quietly fighting the good fight against ignorance and indifference. Enlightening. Inspiring. Encouraging. And doing all this, as they've always done, not because it's their job, but because it's their life.

> *I guide you in the way of wisdom*
> *and lead you along straight paths....*
> *Hold on to instruction, do not let it go;*
> *guard it well, for it is your life.*
> PROVERBS 4:11, 13 NIV

Respecting Privacy

> Gossip needn't be false to be evil—there's a lot
> of truth that shouldn't be passed around.
>
> —FRANK CLARK

*M*aybe there's a little bit of the "Peeping Tom" in all of us. Perhaps that's why we delight in snooping around the most private lives of our most public celebrities. It's what keeps the tabloids in business and keeps those magazine gossip shows on TV.

But wasn't the quality of life a little better—and maybe a little more fun—before the age of tell-all books and unauthorized biographies? Wasn't society somewhat more civil when we maintained a few secrets and kept at least some of our skeletons safely in the closet? I'm not sure our world is better because paparazzi with long lenses intrude into the private sunbathing of Britain's royal family or into the weddings and funerals of well-known personalities who would prefer to be witnessed by only family and close friends.

Carol Channing used to close her nightclub act by inviting the audience to ask questions. Personal questions. One evening a man seated right in front of the stage asked, "Carol, do you remember the most embarrassing moment you ever had?"

Carol responded, "Yes, I do. Next question."

Just because everything about everybody *can* be known doesn't mean it should be.

> *Love does not rejoice at wrongdoing, but finds its joy in the truth. It is always ready to make allowances, to trust, to hope and to endure whatever comes.*
>
> 1 CORINTHIANS 13:6-7 NJB

Speaking Positively

How often misused words generate misleading thoughts!

—HERBERT SPENCER

*O*f all the so-called success secrets, the most important is to be positive. It works in business. It works in personal relationships. Most of us prefer associating with people who are *for* something instead of *against* everything. And it's not that difficult to take a positive approach. So much of our negativism is merely habit.

An easy first step for breaking the habit is to change the way we speak. Whenever possible, instead of saying we're against something we can say what we're for!

If you're a boss, instead of saying to your employee, "Why can't you ...?" change the wording to "What if we did it this way?"

If you're a wife or husband, instead of telling your spouse, "I hate it when ..." phrase it in the positive, "Wouldn't it be better if ...?"

If you're a parent, instead of yelling at your child, "You never do anything around here," why not try, "You know, at times we've had some problems getting things done ..."

These seem like simple changes ... and they are. But the

results from such a positive approach can be positively astounding. Not only do positive people get more done—they have more fun.

In an electrical circuit the positive wire always carries the juice. It's the same in our relationships where the positive person inevitably turns out to be the live wire.

> *Do not let any unwholesome talk come out of your mouths, but only what is helpful for building others up according to their needs, that it may benefit those who listen.*
>
> EPHESIANS 4:29 NIV

The Fudge Factor

> Character is a by-product; it is produced in
> the great manufacture of daily duty.
> —WOODROW WILSON

Not many people live life strictly by the book. Not 100 percent of the time. Because we're all human, we all have what I call a built-in fudge factor. What I mean is we all try to push the limits—at least sometimes. If the speed limit's 65, we figure 70 won't hurt! And is there anyone who hasn't, at some time, tried to squeeze an extra ten minutes out of the parking meter? Or tried to talk a waiter into serving them ten minutes after the restaurant officially closed? Or tried to slip to the front of a line when they thought no one was looking? At a bank? A ball game? A movie? And speaking of movies, did you ever fudge your age up a year or two to get a senior discount—or down so you could get the student rate?

Sometimes a little fudge can leave a lot of egg on our face: Like the student who tried to get through one of those ten-items-or-less checkout counters at a Boston supermarket. Only his basket was loaded. The clerk looked at the full basket, looked at the student, and then said, "Son, I don't know whether you're from M.I.T. and can't read, or from Harvard and can't count."

Just how much can we bend the rules before breaking our character? Asking ourselves that question from time to time is the best way to keep the fudge factor from becoming something worse.

> *You are truly my disciples if you keep obeying my teachings. And you will know the truth, and the truth will set you free.*
>
> JOHN 8:32 NLT

Good Examples

> The secret of discipline is motivation. When a person is sufficiently motivated, discipline will take care of itself.
> —SIR ALEXANDER PATERSON

*H*ow do we motivate our children to be their best?

Have you ever looked at your youngster and thought, "Here's a kid with a hundred acres of possibilities and only a half-acre under cultivation?" It's a challenge faced by teachers as well as parents.

Telling stories from our own misspent youth doesn't always compute. Explaining how much we wish we'd studied harder when we were their age usually provokes a sleepy look and audible yawns. They simply can't understand how our adult lives might be richer and more rewarding had we taken algebra or history more seriously.

Drawing examples from great legends of history doesn't always work either, as one dad discovered when he cited Abraham Lincoln's dedication to learning:

"Son, when Abe was your age, he used to walk ten miles every day to get to school."

And the kid said,

"Yeah, Dad, and when he was your age, he was president."

Our children may ignore what we say, but not what we do: Every time we pick up a book we're showing them that learning matters. Example isn't the best way to motivate. It's the only way.

> *Follow my example, as I follow the example of Christ.*
>
> 1 CORINTHIANS 11:1 NIV

Money Madness

> Money is our madness, our vast collective madness.
>
> —D.H. LAWRENCE
>
> Wealth is like seawater; the more we drink the thirstier we become.
>
> —ARTHUR SCHOPENHAUR

Some people seem predisposed to brooding unhappiness no matter how bright their circumstances. This week I came across a story about two old friends who ran into each other at a social event. One of them looked really depressed, so his friend said, "Man, you look like you're at the end of your rope. What's the matter?"

"Well," the man explained, "Just three weeks ago my aunt died and left me one hundred thousand dollars."

"That's terrific," the friend responded.

Then, with hardly a pause, the other man said, "And just two weeks ago another relative died unexpectedly and left me half a million."

The sympathetic friend muttered, "Unbelievable."

"But that's not all," the man said. "Only last week I won three million dollars in the lottery—all taxes paid."

At this point the friend was really annoyed and he said, "With all this good luck, why in the world are you so down in the dumps?"

And the other guy replied, "Because so far this week—nothing!"

Gratitude is not an automatic response to good fortune. The bigger we are, the greater our capacity for appreciating even life's smallest gifts.

> *How much better to get wisdom than gold,*
> *to choose understanding rather than silver!*
> PROVERBS 16:16 NIV

The Joy of Honest Self-Evaluation

> *Accuracy is the twin brother of honesty; inaccuracy is a near kin to falsehood.*
>
> —Tyron Edwards

*W*e could learn more from our mistakes, if we admitted them. But deficiencies are more easily disguised than acknowledged. A favorite method is the careful choice of words. Consider these examples:

When the owner of a Rolls Royce complained that his car had stalled, an indignant salesman sniffed: "Sir, a Rolls may on occasion cease temporarily to proceed forward. But, sir, a Rolls does not stall."

When a visitor to the Astrodome noticed rain on the seats and commented that the roof leaked, the guide replied in all seriousness, "Madam, the Astrodome does not leak. At times, certain atmospheric conditions cause the glass in the roof to shrink, thereby leaving spaces through which water may enter the building. But the Astrodome does not leak."

Officials in the former Soviet Union were particularly good at such double-speak. Asked to explain why Soviet airlines had more luxurious seats in the fronts of their planes, the official insisted there was no First Class section. After all, they were a classless society. So how did a Soviet citizen get to sit in the better seats? Simple, the bureaucrat explained. They pay more.

A vice doesn't become a virtue simply by changing its description. To honestly solve any problem we first have to honestly admit it exists.

> *I made my sin known to you,*
> *did not conceal my guilt.*
> *I said, "I shall confess*
> *my offence to Yahweh."*
> *And you, for your part, took away my guilt,*
> *forgave my sin.*
>
> PSALM 32:5 NJB

The Joy of Success

> Nature gave us two ends—one to sit on, and one to think with. Ever since then our success or failure has been dependent upon the one we used most.
>
> —GEORGE R. KIRKPATRICK

*H*ave you noticed in a paint department just how many hundreds of colors are available these days? And did you stop to think that despite all these choices there are really only three colors? Red, yellow, and blue? Remember, we learned about those primary colors in grade school. But surrounded by today's innumerable choices, we may have forgotten that every one is nothing more than some combination of red, yellow, and blue.

Well, I got to thinking about all the thousands of books and tapes and lectures on success. It occurred to me that all the formulas and strategies and so-called success secrets are like the colors in the paint store. There are only three primary principles of success: affirmation, attitude, and action. Everything else is just some combination of those three.

Affirmation—what we believe. Attitude—how we feel. Action—what we do.

Despite what seem like endless choices, the fact is, there are no new basic principles of effective living. And there never will be.

Life's most important rules are startlingly simple. If diet and exercise promote a *healthy* life, beliefs, attitudes, and actions determine the quality of life. It's as basic as red, yellow, and blue.

> *The kingdom of heaven is like a merchant in search of fine pearls, who, on finding one pearl of great value, went and sold all that he had and bought it.*
>
> MATTHEW 13:45 RSV

Building Bridges, Not Walls

> *Respect for the sacred personality and natural rights of all men, even while rejecting their errors of mind or life, serves to eradicate vicious antagonisms without surrendering of beliefs or principles.*
>
> —IGNATIUS SMITH

A few years ago I visited a unique commune in Israel cofounded by a Jew, a Muslim, and a Roman Catholic. It brought together young people of all three faiths and cultures so that they could get to know each other. As the kids got acquainted, centuries of hostilities seemed to magically melt away.

How many of our biases could be reduced if we created more friendships across religious and ethnic lines? As American society becomes more diverse and, at the same time, more economically interdependent, such understanding is essential to our nation's survival.

Other countries may be ahead of us. For instance, we have about eighteen hundred American students studying in Japan, while the Japanese have forty-five thousand students studying in the U.S. Throughout their college years, about seventy thousand U.S. students have an opportunity to study abroad. That's less than 2 percent.

But we don't have to go across an ocean to get acquainted with those of other cultures. It may be as easy as going across the street. Getting to know people different from ourselves is one of life's most satisfying experiences. So let's take a chance. The only thing we risk losing is our prejudice!

> *For love of my brothers and my friends*
> *I will say, "Peace upon you!"*
>
> PSALM 122:8 NJB

The Joy of Faithfulness

> *The person who makes a success of living is the one who sees his goal steadily and aims for it unswervingly. That is dedication.*
>
> —CECIL B. DEMILLE

I was master of ceremonies at an awards program for outstanding employees where one honoree had not missed a day of work—or even been late—for forty consecutive years. Amazing, I thought. What an impressive record in an era when reliability seems increasingly rare and devotion to duty sounds like a dusty holdover from an earlier century.

Even Broadway complains that stars are increasingly missing performances. It has been a tradition on stage that the show must go on. And, there are still some pros who've held to that standard:

Sandy Duncan never missed a performance during her two-year run in *Peter Pan*, despite several injuries. She performed some of those flying scenes when she literally couldn't walk.

Lauren Bacall starred in *The Woman of the Year* 513 consecutive times without missing a single show. Raquel Welch later took over the role and appeared 208 times without an absence.

One producer remembers performers working with 105-degree fevers. Today, he says, many younger actors will stay home with the sniffles. And in offices and factories and schools across America, it seems, life imitates art.

A little talent and a good publicity agent might make anyone a star. But only character and a conviction that *the show must go on* will make a person great in any field.

> *Whatever work you find to do, do it with all your might.*
>
> ECCLESIASTES 9:10 NJB

The Joy of a New Beginning

*A*fter nearly thirty years on the local TV anchor desk, my departure from that job was reported in the newspapers as a retirement. I spent the next several months explaining to friends and viewers that this so-called retirement had nothing to do with fishing, rocking chairs, or shuffleboard. It was merely a fork in the road, a passage from one interesting and challenging career to another.

Although considerably younger than Congressman Sam Gibbons, I certainly understood where he was coming from. When he left the United States House of Representatives, Gibbons announced, "This is a mid-life turning point for me." He was seventy-six at the time.

Writing books and broadcasts, delivering speeches, operating a communications business—these keep me busier than TV reporting ever did. Frankly, I'm too busy these days to answer all those questions about, "What's it like to be retired?"

After leaving the White House, President Calvin Coolidge was filling out a membership card for the National Press Club. Under occupation he wrote "retired." Under remarks he wrote "glad of it."

When retirement means gaining a new life—not just giving up the old—we can be glad of it.

> When Abram was ninety-nine years old, the Lord appeared to him and said: "I am God the Almighty. Walk in my presence and be blameless. Between you and me I will establish my covenant, and I will multiply you exceedingly."
>
> GENESIS 17:1-2 NAB

The Meaning of Success

> *I know the price of success: dedication, hard work, and an unremitting devotion to the things you want to see happen.*
>
> —FRANK LLOYD WRIGHT

Success is one of today's hot words. You find the word everywhere—in book titles, magazine articles, advertisements, seminars, and talk shows. And you can hardly find anyone who doesn't want to experience it.

But just what is success? The dictionary definition includes gaining fame and wealth. Most people today would broaden that traditional definition to include happiness and good relationships.

Perhaps no one has come up with a better, more comprehensive, more universal definition of success than Ralph Waldo Emerson. He believed success was:

To laugh often and much;

to win the respect of intelligent people and the affection of children;

to earn the appreciation of honest critics and endure the betrayal of false friends;

to appreciate beauty, to find the best in others;

to leave the world a bit better ...

to know even one life has breathed easier because you have
lived.

This is to have succeeded.

Success ultimately is so personal, only we know if we've
achieved it. Does it matter much that others consider us either
to have failed or succeeded if deep inside we know better?

> *Anyone who loses his life for my sake, and for
> the sake of the gospel, will save it. What gain,
> then, is it for anyone to win the whole world
> and forfeit his life?*
>
> MARK 9:35-36 NJB

Knowing Yourself

> *A humble knowledge of self is a surer road to God than a deep searching of the sciences.*
>
> —THOMAS À KEMPIS

*T*he girl was startled. "I had no idea I looked like that," she told her dad. She had just returned from a restaurant where the walls were covered with mirrors. For some time she'd stared at one of the mirrors, unaware that the image was hers.

People who see themselves on videotape for the first time or hear their voice on audiotape often have the same surprised reaction. "I didn't know I looked like that." Or, "That can't be *my* voice."

And if we're so shocked when we see or hear ourselves as others do, imagine how much more of ourselves we don't really know. Is it any wonder we're frequently asking such questions as, "Why did I make that comment?" Or, "Why did I lose my temper?" We ask those questions because we really don't know who we are. We don't understand our own motives. We likely know more about what makes our car run or our television work than we do about what makes *us* tick.

Self-knowledge is the trickiest, most difficult subject of all. Math we can learn in school. Mechanics we can learn on the job. But knowing ourselves—that's a full-time, lifetime course. And it's never completed. Knowledge is power and knowing ourselves gives us power to shape our own behavior. Without such knowledge we can never find freedom, spontaneity, or happiness.

> God, examine me and know my heart,
> test me and know my concerns.
> Make sure that I am not on my way to ruin,
> and guide me on the road of eternity.
>
> PSALM 139:23-24 NJB

Dream On

> Dream lofty dreams, and as you dream, so shall you become. Your vision is the promise of what you shall at last unveil.
>
> —JOHN RUSKIN

*D*id you dream last night? Chances are good you did, even if you don't remember. But what's more important is whether you dream today with your eyes open. It's the dreams we conjure up while awake—the dreams we choose—that make the biggest difference in our lives.

When a patient complained to his doctor that he had a recurring dream that he was a Middle Eastern sheik with a magnificent harem, huge oil fields, more money than he could spend in a lifetime, and a marvelous physique, the doctor said, "So, what's your problem?" And the patient replied, "I keep waking up."

The good thing about a dream we create is that we don't have to wake up from it. We can pursue it. Achieve it. Turn it into reality. Every important achievement in the history of the world and every significant thing you and I have ever accomplished, began as a dream. A dream while we were awake. A daydream.

Dreams have power. And to go through life with no dreams is to be forever asleep to life's most exciting possibilities.

> *And afterward, I will pour out my Spirit on all people.*
> *Your sons and daughters will prophesy,*
> *your old men will dream dreams,*
> *your young men will see visions.*
>
> JOEL 2:28 NIV

The Joy of Gentleness

> *It takes more oil than vinegar to make a good salad.*
>
> —JEAN-PIERRE CAMUS

The man was furious as he stormed up to the store's customer service counter. His face was flushed and his voice loud as he slammed the merchandise on the counter and began berating the clerk. I watched her stiffen and immediately go on the defensive.

How much more effective his complaint might have been had he approached the woman with courtesy. Why, I wondered, did he insist on making her an enemy instead of an ally? Perhaps he'd never been taught the power of persuasion. Or the force of empathy.

Human nature being what it is, a request is almost always met with more cooperation than a demand. When a widow in Germany discovered thirteen of her cherished garden gnomes missing, she ran an appeal to the thieves in the local newspaper. Her ad said: "My late husband collected them. Please bring back the gnomes." Sometime over the next weekend, all the gnomes reappeared in her garden.

In Buenos Aires, a nightclub has started hiring women as bouncers. Their theory? Patrons won't hit a woman. When a woman steps in to restore order, generally men won't act aggressively. Men also fear that if a woman does beat them up, they'll never hear the last of it from their friends. And all these lady bouncers are trained in the martial arts.

Never underestimate the effectiveness of gentle persuasion. History's most important and lasting revolutions were led by people of quiet strength who won by the force of powerful ideas.

> *Blessed are the gentle:*
> *they shall have the earth as inheritance.*
>
> MATTHEW 5:4 NJB

Magical Joy

The truest help we can render an afflicted person is not to take his burden from him, but to call out his best energy, that he may be able to bear the burden.

—PHILLIPS BROOKS

*C*ritics call David Copperfield the greatest magician of our time. But like all illusionists, David doesn't reveal everything from the stage. Let me take you behind the scenes and expose one of Copperfield's greatest feats. I want to show you the greatest magician's most marvelous trick. I'm going to tell you how he uses his talent to turn despair into dreams and self-pity into self-confidence.

It started with a letter from a young magician. David exchanged several letters with him and eventually the young man sent David an article about himself from the local paper. It showed the young magician in a wheelchair. He'd never mentioned his disability. He never mentioned it to anyone. When he hired himself out to perform, all that mattered was what he could do, not what he couldn't.

This inspired David Copperfield to launch a program, teaching tricks to others with disabilities—bolstering their self-esteem, helping them use unused muscles, improving dexterity and coordination.

Today, Project Magic is in thirty countries around the world with some eight hundred teams of magicians and therapists. David Copperfield has walked through the Great Wall of China and made the Statue of Liberty disappear. But he'll tell you his greatest accomplishment is not an illusion at all: It's making a face light up with excitement and hope. Now that's *real* magic.

> *The Spirit of the Lord is upon me,*
> *for he has appointed me to preach Good*
> *news to the poor.*
> *He has sent me to proclaim ...*
> *That the downtrodden will be freed from*
> *their oppressors,*
> *And that the time of the Lord's favor has*
> *come.*
>
> LUKE 4:18-19 NLT

Look Again

> It is a dangerous and serious presumption, and argues an absurd temerity, to condemn what we do not understand.
>
> —MICHEL DE MONTAIGNE

The more we learn about people and situations, the more we recognize that snap judgments can be dead wrong. When she was a young, novice writer, Marjorie Spiller Neagle spent a summer vacation looking for *local color* to include in the book she planned to write. Her main character was to be a shiftless, lazy sort and she thought she knew just where to find him. When she got there it seemed made to order. Run-down farms. Seedy men. Washed-out women.

And there near an unpainted shack she discovered exactly the character she was looking for—a scraggly-bearded old man in faded overalls, hoeing around a little patch of potatoes while sitting in a chair.

Marjorie headed back to her typewriter, anxious to document this slothful character who wouldn't even stand up to work his garden. But as she turned onto a dirt road and glanced back at the man from a different angle, she noticed a pair of crutches leaning against his chair and one of his empty overall legs hanging limply to the ground. In an instant Marjorie's lazy, shiftless character was transformed into a figure of dauntless courage.

Don't believe everything you see, not unless you've managed to see it from every possible angle.

> *Do not judge, and you will not be judged; because the judgments you give are the judgments you will get, and the standard you use will be the standard used for you.*
>
> MATTHEW 7:1-2 NJB

The Greatest Scandal

> Only one thing can give unity in the church on the human level: the love that allows another to be different even when it does not understand him.
>
> —KARL RAHNER

*O*ccasionally, a notable Christian leader becomes involved in a scandal and those of us who call ourselves *believers* suddenly feel embarrassed and ashamed. Whatever it involves—money, sex, or some other failure—it sends a shudder through the entire Christian community.

The fact is that followers of Jesus don't stop being human. Even a casual reading of the New Testament provides ample evidence that the disciples weren't perfect. Remember Peter getting so angry he cut off the ear of a Roman guard? And so scared that on the night of Jesus' arrest, he cursed and swore that he never even knew the man?

Remember how ego and pride took over and some of the disciples got into a heated argument about who would sit next to Jesus in his kingdom? (Anyone who's been in charge of seating at today's high-priced charity fund-raising dinners knows human nature hasn't changed much in two thousand years).

Perhaps the ultimate New Testament *scandal* involving a follower of Jesus was his betrayal by Judas. All of these incidents represent a breakdown of individual character, a failure to be faithful. As Paul understood, life for the believer is a constant battle to do the things we should and avoid doing the things we shouldn't. Expecting perfection from ourselves—or others—ignores history, human nature, and the teachings of the Bible.

So, the road of faith will always have a few potholes in it. The Christian life is a process, not a destination. And while scandals involving prominent Christians are disappointing as well as hurtful to the church, they shouldn't surprise us.

But you know what is *really* the biggest scandal of all? I think it's the chronic bickering and fighting that goes on among believers. The arrogant assumption that my view is correct and yours is wrong. That my personal understanding of Jesus is superior to yours. This lack of tolerance—and humility—can have tragic consequences.

A United Nations study of 107 conflicts around the world concluded that 97 of them were racial, ethnic, or religious in origin. Think of that! Ninety percent of the wars, riots, and revolutions going on in the world are triggered by intolerance.

Infighting has fractured the unity of the church from earliest times. So Paul exhorted Christians to overcome their differences with humility. And he saw achieving unity as a source of joy: "If there is any encouragement in Christ, any solace in love, any participation in the Spirit, any compassion and mercy, complete my joy by being of the same mind, with the same love, united in heart, thinking one thing" (Phil 2:1-2 NAB).

Is it any wonder that Jesus himself prayed for the unity of his followers?

> *I ask not only on behalf of these, but also on behalf of those who will believe in me through their word, that they may all be one. As you, Father, are in me and I am in you, may they also be in us, so that the world may believe that you have sent me.*
>
> JOHN 17:20-21 NRSV

The God of Disguises

> *Suppose a man is in hiding and he stirs, he shows his whereabouts thereby; and God does the same. No one could ever have found God; he gives himself away.*
>
> —MEISTER ECKHART

*I*n the early days of our nation, only cattle were *branded*. Today everything is. From our Guess® jeans to our Dell® computers and Little Caesar's® pizza, it's all about name recognition. I remember a news release from the 3M® company when I was still working as a reporter. It was a reminder to all news media that *Scotch® Tape* is a copyrighted brand name, not a generic term for just any cellophane tape. In fact, the company shortly after that began advertising their product, as "Scotch Brand Tape."

Almost daily we read about lawsuits involving copyright infringements on brand names. Companies pay millions of dollars to promote their brands and are quite touchy about any misuse or unauthorized use of the names.

All of this is understandable in the marketplace. Unfortunately, it's an attitude that too often seeps into the church. Sometimes we're as jealous and protective of our religious identification as any corporation is of its product name. Jesus never seemed to be hung up on labels, and I think he would find a lot of our preoccupation with them laughable or pathetic!

Seven years ago, I created a nationally syndicated radio series called *Second Thoughts*. It's a daily, inspirational feature, designed to illustrate the importance of certain life principles. They are principles that work, that make life more effective. Many are principles I learned as a child. They are all based upon biblical teachings.

But *Second Thoughts* is not a religious program. It is heard on more than twelve hundred radio stations around the nation— and the world. Some of the stations are Christian but most are secular. The program has secular, corporate sponsors. It reaches a wide-ranging audience of believers and non-believers. It deals with values about which most thinking people can agree—values solidly based upon biblical truth, but never labeled as such. Values such as treating others the way we wish to be treated—the Golden Rule. Kindness. Humility. Respect. Self-discipline. Purpose. Living for something larger than ourselves. Confronting life's big questions. Self-sacrifice.

The program has gained an audience and great sponsor loyalty because it presents material not otherwise being offered in secular, commercial media. It is Christian principles without the label. It is biblical truth without the brand name. It is a way to get all people thinking about really important issues, whether they're Christians, Muslims, Jews, or people with no religious brand. I believe this attempt to share truth-without-labeling would be very acceptable to Jesus. He was more interested in feeding people than in receiving credit for the meal.

But this approach turned out to be very upsetting to at least one host at a Christian radio station. During an interview, he berated me somewhat mercilessly for not branding my programs with the Christian label. The fact that to do so would have immediately cost us our sponsor and probably 90 percent of our stations didn't bother him. The fact that millions of people no longer would be hearing these Christian principles and biblical truths wasn't important to him. What stuck in his craw was the fact that I was attempting to spread the word without the proper label.

The biggest people I know have the smallest egos. And a God big enough to have created this marvelous universe must have a much smaller ego than we give him credit for. This God, as revealed in Jesus, certainly cares more about content than about packaging. More about healing the sick, comforting the hurting, and feeding the hungry than about brand names.

He works in mysterious ways and, it seems to me, his methods often defy our stereotypes. Sometimes he works through people who don't even believe he exists. Clearly, he works through organizations with names that have nothing to do with recognized religious institutions or causes. It is, after all, God's universe and he isn't bound by our perception or ideas about him and how he should do his job.

Inevitably, he breaks out of the brand names we use in an attempt to contain him. He's always popping up unexpectedly in the AIDS wards, on the mean streets, in the bars and night-clubs and crack houses—all those unchurchlike places where people are hurting. Didn't we see him working, at times, through cartoonist and former Sunday School teacher Charles Schulz in those Peanuts cartoons?

He is a God of many disguises who refuses our parochial attempts to brand him.

> *I myself taught Ephraim to walk,*
> *I myself took them by the arm,*
> *but they did not know that I was the one*
> *caring for them,*
> *that I was leading them with human ties,*
> *with leading-strings of love,*
> *that, with them, I was like someone lifting*
> *an infant to his cheek,*
> *and that I bent down to feed him.*
>
> HOSEA 11:3-4 NJB